Confessions of a L...

With all good wishes

Sheila Cassidy.

Confessions of a Lapsed Catholic

Sheila Cassidy

DARTON · LONGMAN + TODD

First published in 2010 by
Darton, Longman and Todd Ltd
1 Spencer Court
140 – 142 Wandsworth High Street
London SW18 4JJ

ISBN: 978-0-232-52840-4

'Disclosure' taken from *Watching for the Kingfisher* by Ann Lewin, © Canterbury Press,
2009. Used by permission of Hymns Ancient & Modern Ltd. 'The Desert is Fertile' by
Dom Helder Camara. Originally published in French as *Le Desert est Fertile*, Copyright
© 1974. Reprinted by permission of Georges Borchardt, Inc., on behalf of Editions du
Seuil. Kind thanks to Shirley Harriott, for agreeing to the use of John Harriott's poem
'Our World'.

A catalogue record for this book is available from the British Library

Phototypeset by Kerrypress Ltd, Luton, Bedfordshire
Printed and bound in Great Britain by Thomson Litho, East Kilbride, Glasgow

For all the wise and lovely men and women who have accompanied me this far on my journey.

Contents

Acknowledgments   ix

Part I   Some Reflections on Churchgoing   1
Chapter 1   The Lapsing of a 'Good' Catholic   3
Chapter 2   Why Catholics Go to Church –
                and Why They Don't   9
Chapter 3   Does Not Going to Church on Sunday Matter?   17

Part II   Finding God in Humankind   25
Chapter 4   Finding God in Church   27
Chapter 5   Finding God in Individuals   36
Chapter 6   Finding God in Community   43
Chapter 7   Who are the Heathens Now?   50
Chapter 8   Now: Where is Your God?   58

Part III   Finding God in the Written Word   65
Chapter 9   Finding God in the Old Testament   67
Chapter 10   Finding God in the Psalms   76
Chapter 11   Finding God in the Gospels   85
Chapter 12   Finding God in Poetry   97

Part IV   Finding God in the Natural World   109
Chapter 13   This Planet Earth   111
Chapter 14   Living with Creatures   119
Chapter 15   Where the Wild Things Play   127
Chapter 16   God and the Tsunami   135

Part V   Our Response to the Divine   143

Chapter 17   Caring for the Planet   145

Chapter 18   Caring for One Another   154

Chapter 19   Caring for Ourselves   162

Chapter 20   Caring for God   170

Acknowledgments

My grateful thanks are due to Judith Newton, who patiently typed my handwritten manuscript, but also to my good friends Jacky Clift, Carole Evans, Bonaventure Knollys, Martin Sellix, Chris Bromley, Clare Hallward and Neil and Catherine McKenty, who either read manuscripts or sent emails for this Luddite author. Thanks too to Brendan, David, Helen and Will at DLT who have given me such wonderful encouragement. Lastly I thank my friend John Garner, without whose support my life would not be nearly so much fun.

Part I

Some Reflections on Churchgoing

Godhead here in hiding whom I do adore,
Masked by these bare shadows, shape and nothing more,
See, Lord, at thy service low lies here a heart,
Lost, all lost in wonder at the God thou art.

St Thomas Aquinas

Chapter 1

The Lapsing of a 'Good' Catholic

The reader will have gathered, from the title of this book, that I am no longer a practising Catholic: that I am what is known in the Church as a 'lapsed' Catholic. For those unfamiliar with Roman Catholic jargon I should explain that being 'lapsed', for me, means that I no longer attend Mass, and I no longer avail myself of the sacraments, those 'outward signs of inward grace' which sustained me in my earlier years. To my priest friends (of whom I have many) I explain that this is a sort of sabbatical and that maybe I shall return, on my deathbed or before, pulled back to Holy Mother Church by what G. K. Chesterton called 'a twitch upon the thread', that invisible cord by which Catholics are tied to the Church.

My intention in writing this book is not to denigrate Catholicism, which has led, comforted and sustained me for over sixty years, but to shed a light upon the way God is to be found *outside* the Church even more than in it: in nature, in people, in animals, in poetry and in all the wild and wonderful works of the Divine. Francis Thompson, a Catholic poet writing in the late nineteenth century, says it most beautifully in his poem, 'In No Strange Land':

> The Kingdom of God is within you
>
> O world invisible, we view thee,
> O world intangible, we touch thee,
> O world unknowable we know thee,
> Inapprehensible, we clutch thee!

Does the fish soar to find the ocean,
The eagle plunge to find the air –
That we ask of the stars in motion
If they have rumour of thee there?

Not where the wheeling systems darken,
And our benumbed conceiving soars! –
The drift of the pinions, would we hearken?
Beats at our own clay-shuttered doors.

The angels keep their ancient places –
Turn but a stone, and start a wing!
'Tis ye, 'tis your enstrangèd faces
That miss the many-splendoured thing.

But (when so sad thou canst not sadder)
Cry – and upon thy so sore loss
Shall shine the traffic of Jacob's ladder
Pitched betwixt Heaven and Charing Cross.

Yea, in the night, my Soul, my daughter,
Cry – clinging Heaven by the hems;
And lo, Christ walking on the water
Not of Genesareth, but Thames!

I love this poem because it makes sense of my deep intuition that God is everywhere, in everything shining forth, if we only care to look. Some would accuse me of pantheism, the worship of nature, but they would be wrong. What I worship is God the Creator whom I find each day, each moment, in nature. The Jesuits understand this thinking because they talk about 'finding God in all things'. Funnily enough, it was my increasing appreciation of the Divine in nature, people and animals that made possible my lapsing. One day I asked myself in a simplistic sort of way: 'If God is so amazingly present in the world, in my house, my dogs, my garden, my patients, how can he (or she) be *more* present in church, in the "Real Presence"?'

I should explain that the Real Presence is what Catholics believe to be God, Christ, really and truly physically present in the Eucharist. The high point of the Mass is the Consecration, where the priest says over the bread and wine: 'This is my Body. This is my Blood. Do this in remembrance of me.' The bells ring as the priest raises the consecrated Host for the people to revere: it is a moment of incredible awe and wonder and the congregation bow their heads in adoration. Later in the Mass, the priest and his helpers distribute Holy Communion and the people return quietly to their seats to adore the God within them. I always found the receiving of Communion to be a deeply spiritual experience and, for many years of my life, went daily to Mass in search of this closeness to the Divine. This was for me, as it is for so many Catholics, an experience of God Immanent, or, as the Muslims say, 'God is as near as the neck of my camel'. At one stage in my life I rose early, canoed across a river, walked half a mile through a field and then caught a bus in order to attend daily Mass. So how is it that I can leave it behind me? How can I deliberately deprive myself of the Bread of Life, of the Food for the Journey, when it is available daily in the church around the corner?

The answer, I think, is that I no longer believe that God is more present in the bread and wine than he is in the sea, in the mountains, in the gentle alcoholics who greet me as I walk my dogs. Instead, I believe that God is *within* me, that I have only to acknowledge his presence to know him as powerfully as if I had received the bread and wine. This acknowledging of the Divine presence within is called a Spiritual Communion and is much used by devout Catholics who are not able to attend Mass because of distance, illness, or lack of a priest. I had reason to teach this devotion to a group of unhappy Anglican men and women in Venice some years ago when I was leading a retreat for an enterprising venture called 'Retreats beyond Dover', run by a delightful man called Anthony Weaver.

On this occasion, Anthony had engaged me to lead the retreat and a priest to celebrate Mass for the twenty or so Catholic and Anglican men and women who had signed up for what was a sort of holy holiday. The high moment of the day was, of course, the liturgy and most of us assumed that all members of the group would be united in worship. Imagine my dismay (which turned later to fury) when our chaplain made it clear that he could not give Holy Communion to the 'non-Catholics'.

There has been much discussion about 'intercommunion' over the years and my understanding is that in a private ecumenical liturgy such as ours, no 'scandal' could be given (i.e. the onlookers would not be shocked) if those who were not Catholic were given Communion with the Catholics. Father X, however, felt obliged to stick to the letter of the law and said that only baptised Catholics should receive Communion.

I was both surprised and saddened by the reaction of the Anglican members of the group, who felt that they were being denied something enormously precious and important. It was as though we Catholics had slammed the church door in their faces, or demeaned them by counting them unworthy to receive the sacrament. Our priest was unmoved. 'Let them celebrate their own Eucharist,' he said, 'or come up to the communion rail for a blessing'. It did not matter to him that this was an ecumenical retreat and that it was therefore key that worship should be in common.

I felt both ashamed of the Church and angry at the cruel obstinacy of its representative and set out, therefore, to make amends. I explained as best I knew how, the concept of 'Spiritual Communion' and assured my friends that God would be as much present in *their* hearts as in the hearts of those of us who partook of the bread and wine. Alas, I might have not bothered because they were totally unconvinced and still felt deeply deprived. I then did the only thing I could think of, and deliberately refrained from taking Communion myself in an act of solidarity with the disenfranchised. If I had thought of it at the time I might have persuaded all the Catholics to join me; but I didn't and they didn't.

This experience was important in making me question something which had been fundamental to my belief system for over forty years. The Catholic teaching that the Mass and the receiving of the Eucharist was the most important act of my day – that it was the Eucharist which gave me spiritual strength for each day's journey and made me a better, more compassionate person. It is in this context that I feel the need to question what can be understood as a *magical* quality of the Eucharist – the mysterious transforming of the offered gifts into the Real Presence of the Divine. In the context of my Venetian experience I have to ask: were the Catholics who received the sacrament more blessed than those of us who invited the Divine into our hearts? I suspect the answer is no. The Divine is mysteriously present in our hearts anyway and perhaps our personal invitation to him, or her, does not *increase* that presence but rather makes us more aware of it.

Another set of circumstances which has made me question the teaching on prayer and the Eucharist is the sad revelation of the cruelty of the Magdalen Sisters in Ireland to the illegitimately pregnant girls in their care. Up to the 1950s – or perhaps it was the 1970s – this order of religious sisters ran homes for the care of those unfortunate young women disowned by their families who could not stand the shame of their daughters' situation. In a documentary film of these sisters and their charges, I witnessed both physical and emotional cruelty unworthy of any woman, let alone a nun. The girls earned their keep by working in the Sisters' laundry, which was the way the convent supported itself. I read too *The Light in the Window*, by June Goulding, an account of these girls' lives, written by a young midwife who was hired to supervise and help with the births. She was clearly appalled and angered at the treatment these vulnerable young women received at the hands of the nuns.

My question is simple: how could these women, who had given their lives to religion and spent several hours a day in prayer and study of the Bible, behave like this? The same questions, of course, may be asked about the shaming numbers of paedophile priests. As I write, the Holy Father, Pope Benedict XVI, is apologising to Australians on behalf of the Church for the abuse and cruelty suffered by so many innocent children. These guilty priests also had sacrificed career and marriage to serve the Lord. They said Mass daily, received the Eucharist, said their psalms and prayers – and then went off to beat and sexually abuse those in their care.

It was not all of them, of course; many, many of these celibate men and women have lived heroic lives and loved the children in their care as their own. We thank God for these saintly people. But their existence neither negates nor explains the behaviour of the abusers.

A couple of years ago, I talked to one of my Jesuit friends and asked him what he thought. After a while he said that he thought it was the 'spiritual formation' of the young recruits: the novices who underwent special training to prepare them for their life in religion. Formation today is very different, but fifty and more years ago it was considered necessary to 'break' the spirit of the novice in rather the same way as a horse was broken.

This is not the place for a litany of the sins of Novice Masters and Mistresses, but the type of training used was often deeply counter-human, seeking as it did to instil an attitude of unquestioning obedience to the Church and the superior of the community in which they would serve. The attempt to eradicate, or at least suppress, normal human desires has, of course, led to the use of self-flagellation and other extreme methods of self-denial. A classic 'Life' to be found in the older noviciate libraries was that of the Irish priest Father Willie Doyle, who, when driven mad by desires of the flesh, threw himself into a bed of nettles! I remember, too, Father Michael Ivens SJ (an enchanting, gentle pastor and scholar, alas now dead) telling me how the novices had to break the ice on the pool before their compulsory morning swim!

My own eighteen months of noviciate life was not a happy one. This was in the late 1970s and was in no way abusive, but I nevertheless came away feeling as if my face had been deeply scratched and that the whole experience had been somehow worse than prison. A doctor friend of mine 'tried her vocation', as they say, in an enclosed convent also in the 1980s, and emerged much the worse for wear when booted out of the convent at twenty-four hours notice for asking for more time to consider taking her final lifelong vows.

My good friend Anne, however, is wise and jolly and extremely happy in her Carmelite convent, as is another friend who entered a couple of years ago.

Enough. My point is this: hours of prayer, daily attendance at the Eucharist and generous renunciation of sexual love and marriage does *not* necessarily produce kind, gentle, honest, humble nuns and priests. What a pity: and, of course, what a mystery!

Over twenty years ago, when I was a lot more pious than I am now, my niece Lucy, then a young teenager, refused to go to Mass. When I asked her why, she said quite simply: 'I don't get anything out of it'. Now, as I write, this seems to be a very reasonable response but at the time I was quite shocked. As a Catholic child of the 1940s and 1950s, I had been brought up to go to Mass on Sunday whether I liked it or not. No one ever asked me if I *got* anything out of it: I was a Catholic so I went to Mass and that was that. Furthermore, I had been clearly taught that to deliberately miss Mass on Sunday was a *mortal sin* and, if I didn't confess and receive absolution, I would go to hell for all eternity. It was as simple as that, and I, as a 'Good Catholic', never questioned this teaching until a few years ago.

Now, as I sit writing in my friend Clare's house in Maine, I think that this teaching is quite simply crazy. What kind of a monster God would consign a ten-year-old child – or a seventy-year-old woman for that matter – to eternal damnation simply for refusing to go to a religious liturgy? In the next chapter, I propose to take a look at why people go to church; and why they don't. As always, this will be a personal view, happily uncorroborated by surveys and statistics!

Chapter 2

Why Catholics Go to Church – and Why They Don't

When I was a child I went to church because my father, a career Air Force officer, made me. I didn't enjoy it at all, or 'get anything out of it'. I found it long and boring and a difficult place to pray. One day, when I was about eight, I forgot my hat – and all good Catholic girls knew then that they must cover their heads because St Paul had said so, two thousand years earlier. To my surprise and indignation, my father said I couldn't come to Mass without my hat and condemned me to wait in the car (the official Air Force limousine), watched over by the chauffeur.

As I sat sulking in the car, however, I gained far more spiritual insight than I would have done had I been allowed to go to Mass. The first thing I knew was that my father was wrong: he was, poor darling, a very letter-of-the-law Catholic, raised as he had been by the Australian Christian Brothers. I knew, deep in my heart, my middle or wherever one knows these things, that God loved me as much without my hat as with it.

As the years rolled by and I was a young teenager in Australia, I used to spend my summer holidays with my Aunt Isobel, my father's widowed sister. Old enough to roam around Watson's Bay (in Sydney) unchaperoned, I took to visiting the church when it was empty. There, in my shorts and shirt, I sat and gazed at the altar and opened my heart to the Divine. Oh how different this was from going to church on Sunday when the church was heaving with people and it was so hard to be still inside. Years later I took to going to daily Mass, where there was only a handful of people and we could each have a pew to ourselves. I realised then that, if I had a choice, I would go to Mass every day *except* Sunday, when I would have a well-deserved lie-in!

It wasn't until I was in the senior school, at Our Lady of Mercy College Parramatta, that I began to appreciate the way that good liturgy could make me feel. My dearest memories are of when I was a boarder in my final year and we went to Benediction on Sunday evening. Benediction, I should explain, is a short liturgy (now rather in decline) in which a consecrated host is 'exposed' in a fabulous gold vessel called a monstrance. The monstrance displays the host through a little glass window surrounded by rays like the sun and, in the candlelight, it is an awesome and beautiful object to gaze at. Add in the smell of incense, the ascending clouds of smoke and the blissful music of the service and one can be transported into a seventh heaven, reminiscent of the prophet Isaiah's experience in the temple when he had a vision of the Divine:

> In the year of King Uzziah's Death I saw the Lord Yahweh seated on a high throne; his train filled the sanctuary; above him stood seraphs, each one with six wings: two to cover its face, two to cover its feet and two for flying.
> And they cried out one to another in this way,
> 'Holy, holy, holy is Yahweh Sabaoth.
> His glory fills the whole earth.'
> The foundations of the threshold shook with the voice of the one who cried out; and the temple filled with smoke.
>
> Isaiah 6:1–5

These memories of Benediction bring to mind the thought that having something to focus one's attention on makes prayer much easier. Later in my life, at Mass in Plymouth, England, I used to focus on the altar, thereby screening out the other worshippers so I could feel that I was alone with God. When the Bishop decided to refurbish the church (should he have spent the money on good works instead, I ask?), he placed the pews facing each other rather than towards the altar. That meant that one could only see the altar by turning one's neck through ninety degrees (something which gets harder as one gets older!). I was furious because I felt that he had deliberately sabotaged my system of worship. More importantly, the other parishioners were furious too. 'We don't want to look at each other,' they said, 'we want to look at the altar' (where Jesus is, they might have added). The unfortunate parish priest suffered his outraged parishioners' complaints until he could stand it no longer and gave in, turning the pews back to face the altar.

All was well until Cardinal Basil Hume OSB came to visit Plymouth and the Bishop insisted that the pews be put back facing each other, the way they are in monastic abbeys. Cardinal Basil praised the Bishop for his understanding of modern liturgy and, from that time on, the pews in the Cathedral of St Boniface in Plymouth have faced each other. No doubt it didn't occur to Basil, or his Bishop, that in monastic pews you can raise the seat and face the altar; whereas in standard church pews you can sit or kneel or stand but you can't face the altar instead of your neighbour.

All this seems a bit petty but it is illustrative of the way in which decisions in the Catholic Church are often imposed from on high and not discussed or negotiated with the laity.

Returning to the question of focusing as an aid to achieving inner stillness in prayer, I have long found that a single candle in a darkened room is a wonderfully effective way of shutting out the distractions of life. An alternative I have also found helpful is to focus on the crossbar of a window, probably because of its resemblance to the traditional crucifix. I should add here that images of Jesus' tortured body hanging on the cross make me feel profoundly uneasy.

Two different kinds of focusing, learned from the practice of Buddhist meditation, are focusing on the breath and the repetition of a mantra, such as 'Maranatha' – the Aramaic for 'Come Lord Jesus'. I prefer the focusing on the breath, in which one sits relaxed but in an upright posture and, with eyes closed, breathes in through the nose and out through the mouth. The act of observing the sensation of the cold air entering the nostrils soon stills the mind by banishing thought and what Annie Dillard, Pulitzer Prize-winning author of *Pilgrim at Tinker Creek*, describes as 'the mind's muddy river':

> The world's spiritual geniuses seem to discover universally that the mind's muddy river, this ceaseless flow of trivia and trash, cannot be dammed, and that trying to dam it is a waste of effort that might lead to madness. Instead you must allow the muddy river to flow unheeded in the dim channels of consciousness; you raise your sights; you look along it, mildly, acknowledging its presence without interest and gazing beyond it into the realm of the real where subjects and objects act and rest purely, without utterance. 'Launch into the deep' says Jacques Ellul, and you shall see.

The secret of seeing is, then, the pearl of great price. If I thought he could teach me to find it and keep it forever I would stagger barefoot across a hundred deserts after any lunatic at all. But although the pearl may be found, it may not be sought. The literature of illumination reveals this above all: although it comes to those who wait for it, it is always, even to the most practiced and adept, a gift and a total surprise.'

Enough about focusing. We don't go to church to focus on anything or anyone; but it certainly helps if we do it more when we're there.

One of the principal reasons many Christians (Catholics, Anglicans, Methodists and others) enjoy church is the liturgy: the theatre of the service, and especially, of course, the music. I spent a blissfully happy eighteen months living on the periphery of a large Benedictine Monastery, Ampleforth Abbey in Yorkshire. I attended the liturgy, the Divine Office (a collection of psalms and spiritual readings), five times a day when the monastic services were held. Matins, the first prayer of the day, was chanted rather than sung, but had a charm of its own. I loved being a part (not necessarily appreciated by the monks!) of the monastic offering, and shared in my heart their fatigue and discomfort at being up so early in the morning.

After forty minutes of silent personal prayer, the monks returned to their choir stalls and we sang Lauds, the joyous office to greet the new day. There is something completely magical about Gregorian chant, the ancient music of the Church dating back hundreds of years. I love it most sung by monks: their lower voices please my ear more readily than the higher voices of the nuns. I enjoyed the chant when I was a novice too but was irritated and saddened by the fact that my voice was too cracked and unreliable to join in.

Gregorian chant plucks at the strings of my heart, causing it to sing inwardly in a wild ecstasy of delight, and I have a sneaking feeling that it is the music which brings many of the worshippers to church. It is rare to hear Gregorian chant in a parish situation these days, although the old favourite 'Credo III' gets the occasional airing. To my ear, some of the older hymns (and a few of the newer ones) come second best to the ancient chants, though the words of some are a rich source of devotion. A writer can talk more powerfully about God in poetry and hymns than in prose and I often read them to myself at home. I find that many express a theology which chimes with my own and that, of course, feels good.

One that comes immediately to mind is 'Will You Let me Be Your Servant', by Richard Gillard. I love particularly two lines in this hymn:

> I will hold the Christ-light for you
> In the night-time of your fear

because they epitomise for me the heart of my years of work with the dying: the being there as friend and comforter to the patients in both the hospice and the hospital.

What a contrast, too, is the notion of God as servant: the Servant King who washed his disciples' feet to model his way of ministering, his way of being God. It always fascinates me that although the three evangelists, Matthew, Mark and Luke, record the breaking of the bread in their account of the Last Supper, John, the beloved disciple, makes no reference to it, focusing instead upon the washing of the feet and Jesus' mind-blowing teaching about Love:

> Love one another as I have loved you.
> By this shall men know that you are my disciples.
> John 13:34–35

Where has the institutional church gone wrong? Why do Catholics put the Pope on a pedestal and dress him up like a king? Where did they get that from? Surely not from the Gospels. Why do we revere him as the 'Holy Father' and, indeed, what opportunity do we give to him to be holy, locking him up in a palace far away from the people he is called to serve? My ex-Jesuit friend, the Canadian writer and broadcaster Neil McKenty, looked at the Pope on American television last night and said: 'Where are the women?' How come Christ's representative on earth is surrounded by men, and celibate men at that? Roll on the day when Catholic priests may marry and Catholic women become priests. More of that later.

I write this book as Anglicans in the UK are discussing (dare I say, bickering over) whether women should be ordained bishops. I find the arguments and the behaviour of the anti-faction both sad and ridiculous. 'Jesus didn't have women apostles,' they moan. So what? We're talking about over two thousand years ago in Palestine, when the culture and the role of women was so very different to our own time.

In this, the twenty-first century, women are accepted as doctors, lawyers, engineers and even heads of state. In the Anglican, Lutheran, Jewish and Methodist churches, women have been admitted to the priesthood for some time. I have vivid memories of my friend Carolyn Brodribb's ordination in Exeter Cathedral: it was a beautiful and moving event – as indeed are all ordinations. The best moment for me, however, was after the service as I stood outside the cathedral and watched two little girls rush up to one of the women ordinands, who gathered them into her arms. Motherhood and priesthood: what a glorious and fitting combination, for are not mothers mentors, comforters, arrangers of celebrations, chastisers and the ever-present sustainers of the unity of the family? I applaud Housetop, the charity which works for the ordination of women in the Catholic Church: more power to their prophetic elbows.

The subject of women clergy leads me naturally back to the subject of why people go to church. Many people go to church for simple reasons: because they like and respect their priest or minister, for example, and he or she preaches a good sermon. Charismatic or holy ministers will always draw people to church, and that is surely as it should be, even though I was taught that the Mass was the Mass, a fount of grace and spiritual strength whoever said it. When I was in medical school at Oxford I rode my bike a mile or so every morning to attend Mass in the Catholic chaplaincy, when I could have more easily gone to the Church of St Aloysius, which was next door to my college. No one questioned the reasons for my choice of liturgy but I see now that it was because I adored the chaplain, Father Michael Hollings, who was a truly remarkable man.

Michael, who sadly died some years ago, became a life-long friend and mentor. I loved him when I was a student because he was kind and funny and a wonderful listener: always there, both physically and emotionally, for his young flock. He was generous to a degree, providing tea to any student who dropped in and food to any tramp who knocked on his door. Michael continued this hospitality after he left Oxford for a London parish, and I have a vivid memory of him making piles of sandwiches and stirring soup for the men of the road.

Alas, not all priests I have met were like Michael. Our parish priest in Australia once angrily tossed the small change from the Sunday collection on to the road in an effort to make his parishioners more generous. If I'd been older I'm sure I would have delighted in putting fistfuls of the smallest coppers in to the collection the following week. Something else I remember clearly, however, is the sight of the same priest sitting on top of our farm gate, with Rusty the Alsatian snapping at his heels and my mother, who hated the Catholic Church in general and the priest in particular, giggling weakly at his fear and indignity. All of which leads me to the conclusion that priests are men before they are priests, and merit our respect only if they earn it. My hunch is that years of subservient 'yes Father, no Father', derived from the notion that the priest is God's representative on earth, has given the priesthood an aura and mystery that it does not deserve.

In the medical world there is a similar hierarchy, with a mystique attached to those at the top. Perhaps the consultant's pin stripe suit is the equivalent of the priestly dog collar, a sign of authority and superiority. Things, of course, are changing and not all consultants wear 'The Suit', just as not all priests wear 'The Collar'. I personally welcome this trend toward informality because both priests and doctors are, by nature of their calling, servants, as Jesus was a servant and a washer of feet. As Richard Gillard's hymn both begins and ends:

> Will you let me be your servant?
> Let me be as Christ to you.

Another important factor which draws people to church is what the Anglicans call 'fellowship': the meeting of like-minded people for prayer, hymn-singing and good conversation. This kind of community-building can be really good, provided the group formed is open to welcoming the stranger and reaching out to the needy. Parishes of all denominations do wonderful things, such as ministering to youth groups and visiting the bereaved and the elderly. Much of this depends upon the energy of the priest or pastor and his or her ability to lead and energise his or her parishioners. Although I have no figures to prove it, my guess is that Anglican churches are better at this than most Catholic ones – but I could be quite wrong. One of the Catholic arguments for a celibate priesthood is that a man unencumbered by family will be freer to be available to his people. This may be true, but I find the argument that a man or woman supported by his or her family will be emotionally more resilient to the demands of ministry more cogent.

Lastly, or, more correctly, firstly, people go to church to honour God. Clearly religious people have a need to worship and many find the church setting conducive to prayer. I am, no doubt, in the minority in that I find myself more at peace in empty churches than in full ones. Even for me it was not always like this because, as mentioned earlier, I have a deep love of monastic liturgy with its Gregorian chant and beautifully-read scripture. In some ways, my time at Oxford spoiled me for ordinary parish Catholicism, which could never live up to the liturgy at the student chaplaincy or at the Dominican church at Blackfriars. The other issue for me was that I had a deep sense of belonging to the hospital community and had no desire to embrace the church one as well. All these are very personal reasons, and other Catholics or Anglicans will have their own reasons for going or not going to church. My need for formal liturgy has diminished as I have got older and I suspect that I am not alone in this. Maybe my absence from attendance at church is a sabbatical and maybe it isn't, but does it really matter if I find God in other places and in other ways? More – much more – of this later!

Chapter 3

Does Not Going to Church on Sunday Matter?

This, of course, is the question that I asked myself every week when I first started missing Sunday Mass. My 'lapsing' was gradual, and came about because of practical issues rather than spiritual ones. I was working very hard as a senior doctor at the time and had no wish to sacrifice my one lie-in of the week. There was Mass at six o'clock on a Sunday evening, which was fine because it didn't clash with anything important. At some point, however, I took to visiting my brother and his family fifteen miles away on a Sunday afternoon and, after a walk or a trip in his boat, we would gather together for a typical English afternoon tea. Mike always had tea at five and that meant that I had to either rush off at half past five or skip Mass and stay chatting with the family.

At first I felt very guilty, and worried that the wrath of God would descend upon me, but after a while it seemed right to stay with my family whom I saw only once a week. Some of the time I went to the University chaplaincy Mass but then my friend Barry, the chaplain, was sent off to a far away parish by the bishop and I gradually drifted away from church-going. I give you this rather boring detail to make clear that my lapsing had nothing to do with a crisis of faith or an attack of atheism; it was just that, like my niece, I didn't feel I was 'getting anything out' of going to Mass any more, and I came to believe that the church's teaching that deliberately missing Mass on Sunday was a mortal sin was unreasonable, if not ridiculous.

Once I had made that decision, all sorts of seditious ideas occurred to me. I thought of the Irish farming communities of my forbears and the power and authority that the priest held over his parishioners. Of course, many of those priests were good and holy men whose power lay in the fact that they were literate and better educated than the men and women they ministered to. I did wonder, however, if the idea of God being more present in the Eucharist than in the land, the sea and the beasts gave them a certain hold over a simple community. To put it bluntly, God was locked in the tabernacle and the priest held the key!

My question is: *was* God more present in the tabernacle, with its seductive little red light, or was the Servant King outside, tilling the fields, cutting the turf and feeding the babies with his people? God the carpenter, the fisherman, the healer, does not seem to fit comfortably within the confines of a small box, however beautiful the door; whereas El Shaddai, the God of the mountain, and Jesus, the itinerant preacher, seem utterly at home in the open air.

I find it quite scary to write this because I know that I am challenging one of the fundamental teachings of Catholicism, which is held very dear by millions of people throughout the world. Who am I to challenge this teaching? And yet, why shouldn't I? Surely God and his Church are used to questions, and a retired doctor's musings should damage neither.

Returning to the title of this chapter, I repeat my question: does *not* going to church on Sunday *matter*? The answer to this question clearly cannot be a simple yes or no because a number of different people are involved. Perhaps then we should ask: to whom *does* it matter? First and foremost, we must ask: does your or my not going to church on Sunday upset God, the Divine, the mysterious creator of the Universe?; does God get pleasure from us sitting or kneeling in church, trying to concentrate on a service which gives us no joy and no obvious spiritual nourishment? I suspect not. What *God* asks, if we are to believe the Bible, is that we should be kind and just and honest. We should not hurt his earth or his creatures, and we should look after the poor, the sick, the old and the children amongst us. *That,* as I understand it, is what being a good Christian, Jew, Muslim or Buddhist is all about.

My next question is more complex: is *an individual* damaged, spiritually or emotionally, if he or she stops going to church? The answer to this is clear: it depends upon the individual. If this person ceases to cultivate his or her relationship with the Divine, and embraces a life of self-gratification with no care for his neighbour, then yes, he is damaged. The trouble is, life is not nearly as simple as that. Going to church does not necessarily make an individual a better person: it depends upon whether or not he or she takes in and acts upon what is taught. As Jesus said:

'Blessed are they who hear the Word of God and keep it.'

Luke 11:28

It is perfectly possible to go to Mass on Sundays and practise as a Chilean dictator, a mafia boss or a rapist the other days of the week.

So, what are we to do? Should we close down the churches, stop training priests and abandon religion? Of course not; we can only do what most Christians are doing already: try to make our churches places of warmth and hospitality, and our liturgies life-giving and life-changing. One of the great difficulties for pastors is that different people want different things from their churches; by which I mean that Christians can be culturally very different.

The style of service that I personally find helpful these days is a simple Eucharist with a small group of like-minded people. Before I got my dogs six years ago, I was a frequent visitor at a Jesuit retreat house in the Midlands, where I went to pray, to read the scriptures and to talk to one of the priests. I found these visits deeply life-giving, and they suited my way of life as a busy hospital doctor. The liturgies there suited me well too in that they were quiet and reflective, very different from what was available to me in Plymouth.

I loved, too, the liturgy at Ampleforth, set as it was in a cathedral-like abbey, and performed with enormous grace. The music, of course, was wonderful and I have rich memories of singing this Advent hymn:

> O comfort My people and calm all their fear
> And tell them the time of salvation is near
> All mountains and hills shall become as a plain
> For vanished are mourning and hunger and pain.

I love the music of this hymn, but mostly I love the words, so relevant as they are to my vocation as a doctor and to my work with the dying.

Best of all the monastic liturgies were the Easter ceremonies. The Lamentations of Jeremiah, sung solo and unaccompanied in the early morning on Good Friday, would send shivers up my spine, as would the sound of the words 'Lumen Christi' (the Light of Christ), which were sung three times as the priest entered the darkened abbey church. First one candle would be lit from the Paschal candle, then another and another, until the church was glowing with candlelight, symbolising the light of Christ in the world. (Then, alas, they turned the lights on for safety reasons and the magic was gone!)

Clearly this was a good emotional experience for me and hopefully it strengthened my faith. Other people, however, are culturally very different. I feel at home in an Anglican cathedral liturgy but, frankly, cringe when I see American Pentecostal services on the television. The people involved in such services, however, clearly enjoy their worship and it makes them feel closer to God. 'In our Father's house there are many mansions' – room for plainchant, for Negro spirituals and for rock music. All we can hope is that the walls are soundproofed or there will be serious trouble in heaven!

Another of my concerns about missing Sunday Mass was whether or not I would upset the parish priest, or give 'scandal' to other members of the congregation. I came to the conclusion, however, that even if the priest cared he would get over it and those parishioners who missed me would probably pray for my conversion.

Lastly, there is the question: 'what has abandoning church-going done to me personally?' Am I the poorer for this loss of the Eucharist, and have I strayed from the path of righteousness? My answer to this would be a definite '*No!*' because I feel that, as one door has closed for me, so many others have opened: my experience of Christianity is not only wider and deeper, but also infinitely more joyous. It is this joy that moved me to embark upon this book, in an attempt to share the riches I have found.

I should explain at the outset that there has been a radical change in my way of life since I retired from work at the hospital eight years ago. Up until August 2002, I worked full time in a big cancer treatment unit, seeing breast cancer patients in the clinic and anyone who needed emotional help in our drop-in support centre, The Mustard Tree. I truly loved the patient work, though I got tired and hassled like everyone else. What I didn't like was the rush to get to work on time, the struggle to find a parking place and the endless piles of paperwork which called for my attention. The other thing I didn't like was the inevitable tension between different members of staff. I fell out early on with the woman counsellor appointed to form a team of volunteer counsellors for the patients – something that I thought of as my job. These kinds of differences of opinion and outright hostility are very common in hospitals, just as they are in other institutions (including convents) where strong-minded men and women encroach upon each other's territory. (When I wrote my thesis for my psychotherapy qualification, I chose this subject of conflict in the work place and had a fascinating time reading around the subject.)

Suddenly, on my sixty-fifth birthday, my life as a doctor ended. I could get up when I liked, drink coffee by the sea, write another book and learn to paint. Greatest of all these joys was the fact that I could have a dog! My Chow-chow puppy, Anka (to 'anchor' me to Plymouth), had in fact arrived a month or so before my retirement, being ready for homing towards the end of May. He was, in part, the gift of my close colleagues, whom I loved and love to this day. He cost a lot of money (and still does) but I would rather live in a bed-sit on bread and water than part with him or his sister Mollie, a fabulous black Chow bitch who joined us in October, a week after I had had a bilateral mastectomy for breast cancer. I should explain to the uninitiated that Chows are large, woolly dogs, descended from the arctic wolf (and possibly from bears), and are definitely not to be confused with Pomeranians, which are vaguely similar in design but much smaller! They are stunningly beautiful animals and invite endless comments from passers-by when we promenade upon the sea front each day. They are, however, also extremely stubborn, wilful and given to running off to explore some important scent. They are, in fact, hunting dogs and are definitely not to be trusted with cats, squirrels, sheep or joggers!

I have no doubt that all these benefits of retirement have made me a happier and more relaxed person, but they have also impacted upon my spiritual life in that I have become much more aware of, and grateful for, the Creator and the world which he, or she, created.

What has happened, I think, is that I have slowed down (as one does with age and leisure) and become much more 'contemplative' in my approach to life. When I was thinking about becoming a nun I had to choose between a 'Contemplative' order and an 'Active' one. I should explain that I was tormented by a sense of calling to Religious Life from my last year at school until I exorcised it for ever by 'trying my vocation' in my forties. The 'Active' orders, like the Sisters of Mercy or the Jesuits, live in the community and do good works such as nursing or teaching, fitting their prayer into the spaces between their good deeds. For the Monastic, or so-called 'Contemplative', orders, the theory is that prayer is central and work secondary. A Sister teacher will rise early to pray, work all day in the classroom and say her prayers wearily at night. The

Carmelites or Benedictines, on the other hand, rise early or even in the middle of the night to pray, and interrupt what they are doing for Lauds, Midday Prayer, Vespers and Compline. Their prayer *is* their work and their tasks are done without idle talk. The idea is that they should mull over and reflect upon what they have read or heard of the scriptures – the Word of God – and raise their hearts and minds to God in praise and gratitude. That, at least, is how it's supposed to work. Either way of life suits some people wonderfully well while others somehow wither emotionally and never reach their full potential.

When I entered a monastic order in my early forties, I became deeply unhappy and quite unlike my normal exuberant, and somewhat irreverent, self. It wasn't that I was bored but, rather, terribly lonely for kindred spirits and the dialogue, light and serious, which had hitherto been integral to my life. Our recreation period in the evening was in some ways the worst moment of the day as we sat around a table knitting or sewing and making polite conversation. My sister-in-law, Pat, hit the nail on the head when she described it as being 'like a cocktail party without the booze!'.

There was lots about convent life that I loved; the liturgy and the silence and the constant exposure to the scriptures were meat and drink to me (although not as aesthetically pleasing as the deep voices of the men at Ampleforth!). What did not suit me, however, was the largely unspoken discipline, which produced in me a constant fear of doing the wrong thing. I was absurdly afraid of the Novice Mistress who, though ten years my junior, had a great air of authority. In some ways it was similar to the interpersonal tensions of the workplace, with the one difference that we couldn't go home at the end of the day and put up our feet in front of the telly!

Now that my convent years are well behind me, I understand the word 'contemplative' in a wider sense. I prefer to talk about Active and Monastic religious orders rather than Active and Contemplative ones, because contemplation is a virtue which is certainly not confined within the walls of convents and monasteries. To contemplate, in its ordinary sense, is *to observe*: we contemplate a plan of action, a beautiful scene or the devastation that follows a tornado. Contemplation, in its narrower, spiritual sense, is to observe the footprints of the Divine; to sit, poised, waiting for the crack of a twig or the rustle of leaves to indicate the Presence. If this rather poetic language leaves you baffled, let me try once more to explain. Contemplation is a practice in which a person stills mind and body, emptying the mind if possible or ignoring the ceaseless flow of thought and chat, opening himself or herself to the presence of the Divine. This is something that can be done in church or at home, gazing at the mountains or sitting in a train. It is not something you do while driving a car or performing surgery, but it is perfectly possible to do it while 'tuning out' a television programme others are watching.

This practice of contemplation can lead to an increased awareness of the Divine Presence in all things. As the Jesuit poet Gerard Manley Hopkins wrote, over a hundred years ago:

> The World is charged with the grandeur of God.
> It will flame out, like shining from shook foil;
> It gathers to greatness, like the ooze of oil
> Crushed.
> From 'God's Grandeur'

I seem, once more, to have strayed somewhat from the stated theme of this chapter so let me end by saying that I do not believe that I personally am a worse or a less spiritual person for having abandoned church-going. Furthermore, when I admit to my Catholic friends that I no longer go to Mass I find that many of them share my 'lapsed' condition.

Part II

Finding God in Humankind

The tragic beauty of the face of Christ shines in our faces.
Daniel Berrigan

Chapter 4

Finding God in Church

Having spent the last three chapters talking about *not* going to church, it seems right and proper to explain that I am not suggesting that God has abandoned the Church, but only that I, personally, find the Divine more accessible outside it, or when it is empty. I should clarify once and for all (for the reader and also for myself) just what I mean by the word 'church'. We have churches as *buildings* for communal worship, the Church as *an institution*, the *body of all the faithful* and church *services*.

Starting with churches as *buildings*, I should say at once that I think that many are wonderful for both public and private prayer. There is something about the empty space of churches that instils in many beholders, myself included, a sense of awe. The bigger and the emptier the church, the more awestruck I feel.

The wonderful French Cathedrals of Chartres and Reims give me a sense of wonder, as do our English cathedrals. And one of the most magnificent buildings I have seen is the Hagia Sophia mosque in Istanbul: a fabulous church built by the Christians but taken over by the Muslims. It is a towering space with massive domes, and it is said that the Emperor Constantine, when he saw it for the first time, felt that he had crossed the threshold of heaven.

So what is happening when we experience such awe? My guess is that there are several things taking place, but one of particular note is what I call the mountain, or sunrise, effect. We humans can kid ourselves that we are in control of our world as we drive our cars and fly in our aeroplanes, but when confronted by an enormous and beautiful building or a range of mountains emerging from the mist, our hearts soar and we are minded of the Infinite.

In my experience, a sense of awe is one of the most powerful stimuli to prayer, because it gives us a momentary intuition of the Divine, that there is a power or force beyond ourselves. This is surely why men and women risk their lives to stand at the summit of a mountain and watch the sun come up: they are searching for what is called a peak experience, a moment of ecstasy and connection with the Universe.

Empty cathedrals make me want to throw myself down on the floor in an act of adoration, but full ones can be good in a different way. I remember vividly an evening in the Cathedral in Santiago, Chile, when Cardinal Silva said Mass for 5,000 people after he had returned from Rome. For me, the peak moment was when we sang the Spanish version of Beethoven's *Ode to Joy*:

> Eschucha hermano La Cancion de la Alegria, El canto alegre que espero un nuevo dia. Ven canta, venia cantando, vive sonando el nuevo sol en que los hombres van a hermanos.

Translated, it goes:

> Listen brother to Song of Joy, the song which heralds a new day. Come, singing, live dreaming of the new sun, a world in which all men shall live as brothers.

This celebration took place during one of the hardest years of the military dictatorship, during which the Catholic Church became both a symbol of hope and a powerful source of practical aid to a suffering people. It was the wonderful courage and simplicity of the Church at that time which drew me like a magnet back to Chile after the Coup, for I saw something Christ-like in those churchmen and churchwomen and was determined to be a part of their struggle. Perhaps the Church is at its purest in times of persecution or disaster, when it has no time or inclination to squabble about sex, gender and ritual!

Another way the word 'Church' is used is when speaking of the *institution*, sometimes piously referred to as 'Our Holy Mother the Church'. Our Holy Mother is, in reality, the Men in Rome, the all-male body of priests, bishops and cardinals who work in the Vatican and write the rules by which 'the faithful', the lay Catholics like myself, are supposed to abide. When Catholics speak of 'the Church' they generally mean the *Catholic Church*, just as when Anglicans use the word they generally mean the *Anglican Church*. When outsiders talk about 'the Church' they probably mean the Christian Church, lumping Catholics and Anglicans, Methodists, Baptists and all the other denominations together! In this book, I shall be talking mainly about the Catholic Church, with which I am most familiar, and the Christian Church as an amalgam of all the men and women who believe in the God who became man and lived amongst us.

It is the Catholic Church as an institution which we Catholics love to hate. I suspect that this is particularly true of the more liberal and educated Catholic women who rail constantly at the male-dominated and sexist nature of their church. Most of us move from an attitude of acceptance in our childhood to take on an increasingly questioning stance. Take the Church's teaching on contraception, probably the most hotly debated issue of all: the fact that its use is forbidden makes life for married couples incredibly difficult. The Church teaches that sex is primarily for the procreation of children, and if a couple do not want more children (it is assumed they will have *some*) then they should abstain from intercourse. I suppose that's one way of looking at it, and it clearly seems logical to a celibate, male clergy! Most of us, however, would say 'rubbish!' Of course the sexual act leads to the procreation of children, but it is also integral to the married state. The pleasure, comfort, relief of tension and consolidation of love between partners that it brings is also a vital part of the spousal relationship. How *dare* the men in Rome manipulate women into having more children than they can emotionally or physically care for? Even more important than its impact upon married couples is the issue of forbidding the use of condoms in those countries where HIV is rife and multiple sexual partners the norm.

Two more 'hot' contemporary issues are those of whether Catholic priests should be allowed to marry and whether there is a valid argument against the ordination of women. If we take the issue of married clergy first, I can only say that I don't understand what is standing in the way of their being allowed, particularly as Rome has accepted into the priesthood married Anglican clergy who wished to become Catholic. (The fact that many of these men 'converted' when the Anglican Church started ordaining women makes me very cynical about Rome's pragmatism.) During the thirty odd years since I returned from Chile, I have preached in a great many Anglican churches and Cathedrals, and, in the course of that, met many vicars and their families. Sometimes the pastor's wife has been actively employed in the parish, sometimes busy with small children and sometimes occupied with her own career. I never once met an Anglican clergyman whom I thought would be a happier or better priest if he were celibate. What, I wonder, are the men in Rome thinking about? Do they *know* any Anglicans, I wonder? Have they ever stayed the night in an Anglican family home? Met the vicar's wife and his children? If they haven't, then they should! Perhaps they think that having sex makes a priest unclean, and unfit to celebrate the Eucharist. You could, just as well, say that having sex makes 'a surgeon' unclean and he should not operate on his patients!

Similarly, if women can be doctors, lawyers, judges and engineers, it seems to me outrageous to say they are not emotionally suited to the priesthood. It is interesting to examine the priestly tasks in the light of whether or not a woman could manage them. Saying Mass, administering the sacraments, managing the church finances, listening to sad, lonely, worried people: which of these priestly tasks do the hierarchy think too difficult for a woman? I rest my case.

Perhaps it is because women are intermittently 'unclean' because of their periods, or unstable because of PMT. Are those valid reasons? All I can say is that her womanhood did not stop Margaret Thatcher from being Prime Minister, nor Mother Teresa from setting up an organisation for care of the dying poor in India. It is to be hoped that the men in Rome are aware of the lives and dedication of women like my friend Carolyn, an ex-social worker ordained in her 50s, who runs four parishes, looks after her grandchildren one day a week and organises regular days of prayer for men and women hungry for silence and the Word of God.

Having been somewhat negative about the male hierarchy, I would like to pay tribute to the extraordinary generosity of the thousands of priests and nuns who serve the people of this country and the needy all over the world. Many come from religious orders and are therefore, theoretically, part of the institutional Church. I have *so many* friends in Religious Life, from outspoken American women missionaries to quiet and learned Benedictine and Jesuit priests who have guided me so gently and wisely over the years. My love of, and gratitude to, these dedicated men and women is enormous, for without them I would surely have lost my way.

The third of my groups which fits under the word 'church' is the *body of all the faithful* – all the millions of men, women and children who think of themselves as 'Catholic'. Catholics are, I am sure, no better and no worse than other Christians, Muslims, Buddhists or Atheists. We are all, what ever our label, pilgrim peoples, wounded and healthy, mostly doing our best, though sometimes stupidly or wickedly doing things which damage each other or the planet.

One of the things that make me believe in a loving God is the incredible goodness of so many people. Some are already canonised as saints, like Maximilian Kolbe, who took the place of a married man condemned to starve to death by the Nazis. Others work in developing countries in nursing or medicine, like my friend Sister Bridget, who worked in Rwanda in a bush hospital. There are those who work in the field of human rights, caring for HIV sufferers, the elderly, the mentally ill, the homeless and so on. Robina Rafferty worked for years at CHAS, the Catholic Housing Aid Society, while Julian Filochowski headed up CIIR, the Catholic Institute for International Relations. These are the Catholics whom I know and admire. I could go on and on, listing the Anglican and all the non-denominational Non-governmental Organisations and other charities – *Médecins Sans Frontières* is one I would like to have worked in, as is the Medical Foundation for the Care of Victims of Torture; alas, one can't do everything. I can only emphasise the myriad of good works which shine like candles in a world of wars, poverty, natural disasters and corruption.

The last of my categories of 'church' in which we are likely to find God, is the liturgy – the readings, songs and prayers which go to make up what we call a religious *service*. As I mentioned earlier, there are wide cultural variations in what different groups of people find conducive to prayer. Some of us find 'happy-clappy' celebrations cringe-making, while others would find monastic or Anglican cathedral services pompous and boring.

A word about the public reading of scripture: in the Anglican Church there are those who will tolerate nothing but the Authorised Version, the beautiful but often archaic and obscure text translated in the reign of King James. A number of modern translations are more accessible to the reader but are written in a very prosaic, less beautiful literary style. It is not my task here to judge one translation as better than another, even if I were equipped to do so. Instead I want to write about the importance of listening to and 'hearing' – i.e. absorbing the Word of God as presented in the scriptures them.

I think one of my difficulties in enjoying parish liturgy is that I don't always 'hear' the Word. I suspect, too, that I am not alone in this. It is all too easy, especially if the reader is not very skilled, to let one's mind wander until it is jolted back by the ending: 'This is the Word of the Lord.'

The fault here is mostly mine and I remember back to monastic days when my mind was less cluttered and the text superbly read so that listening was a truly spiritual experience.

I have, as a precious legacy from my days at Ampleforth and the convent, a certain familiarity with the scriptures, both old and new. My favourite texts come mostly from the Old Testament, especially the prophets, with Isaiah as the most loved. Each Advent, at the Mustard Tree carol service at Buckfast Abbey, I am allowed to read the text:

> The people that walked in darkness
> have seen a great light;
> On those who live in a land of deep shadow
> a light has shone.
> You have made their gladness greater,
> You have made their joy increase;
> They rejoice in your presence
> as men rejoice at harvest time,
> as men are happy when they are dividing the spoils.
>
> For the yoke that was weighing on him,
> the bar across his shoulders,
> the rod of his oppressor,
> these you break as on the day of Midian.
>
> For all the footgear of battle,
> every cloak rolled in blood,
> Is burned,
> and consumed by fire.
>
> For there is a child born for us,
> A son given to us
> And dominion is laid upon his shoulders;
> And this is the name they give him:
> Wonderful, Counsellor, Mighty God,
> Eternal Father, Prince of Peace.
>
> Isaiah 9:1–6

For me, for many years, the people who walked in darkness were the Chileans suffering under a military dictatorship, and I prayed for their liberation. Now that they are free my mind turns to Darfur, with its desperate raped women whose husbands have been slaughtered along with their cattle. Everywhere it seems there is violence and killing, even on the streets of London and many of the larger cities of the United Kingdom where I now live. How desperately the world waits for an end to the carnage and for a flowering of peace. The scriptures can give us so much if we will only let them: hope, encouragement, wisdom and a rule for living.

I end this chapter on the Church with another passage from the book of Isaiah, in which, in the name of the Lord, the prophet rants against hypocrisy in religious observance unaccompanied by compassion and justice:

'What are your endless sacrifices to me?' says Yahweh.
'I am sick of holocausts of rams
and the fat of calves.
The blood of bulls and goats revolts me.
When you come to present yourselves before me
who asked you to trample over my courts?
Bring me your worthless offering no more,
the smoke of them fills me with disgust.
New Moons, Sabbaths, assemblies -
I cannot endure festival and solemnity.
Your New Moons and your pilgrimages
I hate with all my soul.
They lie heavy on me,
I am tired of bearing them.
When you stretch out your hands
I turn my eyes away.
You may multiply your prayers,
I shall not listen.
Your hands are covered with blood,
wash, make yourselves clean.
Take your wrong-doing out of my sight.
Cease to do evil.
Learn to do good,
search for justice,
help the oppressed,
be just to the orphan,
plead for the widow.'

Isaiah 1:11–17

It is, of course, easy to pass off this talk of bloody sacrifice and burned offerings as relevant only to a past age and an alien civilisation. If one re-works the passage, however, to fit our contemporary situation, the words have a power for today. I ask forgiveness from the outset for taking liberties with Holy Writ:

'What are your endless liturgies to me?' says the Lord.
'I am sick of your sung masses your novenas and your benedictions.
Who asked you to trample all over my church?
Bring me your worthless offerings no more.
The smoke of incense fills me with disgust.
Feast Days and Sunday, synods and bishops' meetings –
I cannot endure festivals and solemnity,
Your Holy Days and your pilgrimages
I hate with all my soul.
They lie heavy on me,
I am tired of bearing them.
When you stretch out your hands
I turn my eyes away.
You may multiply your prayers
I shall not listen.
Your hands are covered in blood.
The children you abused are damaged forever
Wash, make yourselves clean.
Take your wrongdoing out of my sight.
Cease to do evil.
Search for justice.
Cherish the earth,
Take heed of global warming,
Care for your mentally ill and your men of the road.
Help the oppressed,
Be just to the orphan.
Plead for the widow and HIV sufferers
Give money to help earthquake victims,
Join Amnesty International
Be good to the asylum seekers amongst you;
Visit the old and the lonely,
The bed-bound and the bereaved.
Remember Jesus' last message

On the night before he died
"I give you a new commandment:
Love one another;
Just as I have loved you,
You also must love one another.
By this love you have for one another,
Everyone will know you are my disciples" '

My last word about finding God in church must be about the music. I have already written of how Gregorian chant fills me with a sense of the Divine, but there are hundreds, if not thousands, of hymns that nourish our souls and remind us of the Gospel message. Some reach us by the quality of their music; I have to admit to choosing 'Jerusalem' for the call signal on my first mobile telephone – alas, it is no longer available and I miss the tune and its associations. Others have words which become branded on our hearts or open up new areas of understanding of our faith.

Many years ago, while at Mass in Florida, I was thinking about a priest I knew who had AIDS. I was, in particular, wondering if God would forgive him for the breaking of his priestly vows (what a pious prig I must have been back then!). Anyway, my ruminations were interrupted by a hymn which I had never heard before:

> There's a wideness in God's mercy
> Like the wideness of the sea;
> There's a kindness in his justice
> Which is more than liberty.
> For the love of God is broader
> Than the measure of man's mind;
> And the heart of the Eternal
> Is most wonderfully kind.
>
> F. W. Faber

The love of God is broader than the measure of man's mind: that says it all, I reckon.

Chapter 5

Finding God in Individuals

I started to call this chapter 'Finding God in the Goodness of People', but realised that it sounded as though God is *only* to be found in the virtuous, which is quite simply not true. However, there are some exceptional people, whom I would call 'icon people' because God – the Divine – is so apparent in what they do and in the persons they are. I call to mind two of my mentors: Michael Hollings, of whom I have already written, and the French Canadian, Jean Vanier, who is the founder of L'Arche, a movement for the care of handicapped men and women. What was it that drew me to these men? Looking back, I think it was a delightful amalgam of gentleness, humour, wisdom and, above all, kindness. It was not that they were 'soft' – no indeed! They were both men of steel, of integrity, of vision and tenacity.

Upon reflection, I suspect that they, and others of my icon people, had – or have – much in common with Jesus of Nazareth. I do not mean to be blasphemous here: Jesus was the Son of God, but as a carpenter, itinerant preacher and healer in Palestine, he was truly human, and not yet the Christ.

I find it interesting that the qualities of these men which drew me to them, are more of character and personality, not of an overwhelming piety. Of course Michael and Jean prayed – how else could they sustain the life of endless giving to which they were called? Their devotion, however, was a private matter unless they were asked to share it in a public liturgy or a small group setting.

In my student days at Oxford, I came to know Michael Hollings well. I remember vividly our first meeting: I was languishing in the college infirmary with a chest infection and he came to visit me. One minute I was lying miserably in bed and the next minute I was being asked tenderly by a tall stranger how I felt. What I felt was amazement and inner warmth that someone of his stature should *care* enough to visit me. The previous chaplain, whom I had met, rather than known, in my first year, was Monsignor Valentine Elwes, a charming but somewhat distant man who declared himself happy to see undergraduates 'by appointment'.

Goodness, how Michael breathed life into the chaplaincy, inviting us to drop in to see him any time and feeding us when we were hungry, whatever the time of day. His human warmth and availability became legend, so he became a very hard act to follow as a chaplain. When I qualified as a junior doctor in 1963, I was unable to go home for Christmas so Michael invited me to share his dinner, joining with a motley crew of people who had nowhere else to go. There were lonely women, depressed dons and men of the road, and between us we celebrated the feast in some style.

This welcoming of the lonely and the unloved was one of Jesus' outstanding characteristics, and his followers are usually drawn to emulate him. My most precious moments with Michael, however, were those I spent with him in the early morning as he prayed in silence before the altar in a cold and unlit church. Trying, I suppose, to learn from him, much as the disciples did with Jesus, I sat for half an hour trying to pray while Michael remained huddled in his black cloak in his place at the side of the altar. It was hard for me, at twenty-one, to still myself before God, but I did my best, no doubt as Michael was doing his.

Sharing a time of prayer with Jean Vanier was also a rich experience. Jean himself was, I think, originally a disciple of Père Thomas Philippe, a French Dominican priest, who persuaded him to provide a home for two adult men with what are now called 'learning difficulties'. From this small beginning grew Jean's life's work: the movement of L'Arche – the Ark – that provides home and loving care for hundreds of intellectually-wounded men and women throughout the world.

When he is not visiting L'Arche homes in India, Africa, or Europe, or giving retreats and talks, Jean is based in the village of Trosly-Breuil near the French town of Compiègne. Trosly-Breuil is the organisational heart of L'Arche and is home to a number of individual houses for people with different needs. At one time I used to visit Trosly every few months, to meet with Jean and take time out with God. The celebration of the Eucharist for the community (both handicapped and carers) by Père Thomas was a focal point for everyone, but the best moments for me were the evening prayer time, said *en famille* in each separate house. Jean's 'family' when he was in L'Arche was in a community called La Val Fleuri, which was home to around twenty moderately disabled men. After the evening meal was finished, we would gather as a group in the sitting room, the young carers sitting with the most vulnerable of the men. A candle was lit, the lights dimmed and silence would descend upon a previously talkative group. The prayers said were simple and a hymn was sung, often a little discordantly; then came the individual supplications, which were often extremely touching. I can still hear in my heart the voice of Bernard, a man in his forties, praying for 'mon père et ma mère qui sont au la ciel'.

My most memorable liturgy in L'Arche, however, was the celebration of Holy Thursday, the Last Supper, when we re-enacted Jesus' washing of the disciples' feet. When this ceremony is performed at Ampleforth (and no doubt elsewhere), the washing is inevitably a token one. The person whose foot is to be 'washed' takes off one shoe and sock and the celebrant pours a little water over a very clean foot, patting it dry with a pristine white towel. The foot washing at L'Arche, however, was very different. We sat in a circle and, one by one, took off both shoes and socks. When our turn came, our feet were plunged, one after the other, into a plastic bowl of warm soapy water and gently but thoroughly washed. Once clean they were towelled dry, great attention being paid to the spaces between the toes. To have one's feet washed and dried with such tenderness is to know oneself loved and respected; I expect that is why Jesus did it!

'Icon people' such as Michael and Jean are few and far between, but we can still get a glimpse of the Divine in the kindness of good people. Caryll Houselander, a woman writing during the Second World War, had a powerful experience of the unseen God while travelling on the underground railway in London. Quite suddenly, she 'saw' Christ in each and every person. I have never experienced such a revelation, but my heart has been warmed more times than I can remember by some of my cancer patients. I am moved particularly by the love of elderly men for their frail and dying wives: the tenderness with which they care for their loved one's most intimate needs. Another moment of awareness was when I saw Andrea, a young nurse of around eighteen, as she sat quietly holding the hand of an old man who was dying, because he had no family to keep vigil with him.

It is all very well for me to wax lyrical about encountering the Divine in good people, but what about the ones I dislike or despise? I will not even pretend that I find encounters with those whom I dislike pleasant, let alone a source of moments of spiritual enrichment, but I still learn from such people, even if it is only that I am sometimes as mean-hearted and biased as they! Caryll Houselander thought about this as well, for she wrote that in her vision she saw evil people as dead, waiting for the coming of Christ and the resurrection.

As a psychotherapist, I have a different, more pragmatic take on those who do evil deeds. Knowing, as I do, the impact of abuse or lack of love in childhood, I see such people as the victims of often unwitting parental violence. As it says in Philip Larkin's famous poem: 'They fuck you up, your mum and dad.' Or, as Jesus said, 'the sins of the fathers are visited on the children'.

It is, of course, not always right to blame the parents for their children's misdeeds, because some evil men and women come from loving parents and good stable homes. More often than not, however, there have been problems with drug abuse or alcohol addiction, with victims being influenced by 'bad company' or older villains. There are also the psychopaths, men and women with an incomprehensible love of cruelty and violence.

Then there are the men corrupted by power, who starve, torture and trample upon their people. Today, our minds go instantly to Zimbabwe and Darfur, but the leaders of these suffering regions are only the current examples in a long history of wounded, cruel and evil dictators. I have no answer to this problem of evil and can only pray, with Caryll Houselander, that the tombs of their dead souls are broken open by the Light of Christ.

Even as I write it, I know this is 'religious speak', inspiring to some and nauseating to others. Despite our differences in language, we all want the same: that they should, in the words of Isaiah, 'cease to do evil and learn to do good'.

Returning to my subject of finding God in people, I am reminded at once of one of my favourite *theophanies* – experiences which show forth the Divine – and that is the subject of spiritual calling, or *vocation*. Some years ago, I began a book on 'call' and had a wonderful time reading the biographies of a number of men and women who felt called by God to embark on a particular mission. I believe that this is in no way an uncommon phenomenon, though not all calls are as crazy and flamboyant as others. A favourite vocation story among Catholics is the story of Thérèse of Lisieux, piously known as 'the Little Flower'.

Thérèse was born into a devout French family in the late nineteenth century, and followed her three older sisters into a Carmelite convent at the age of fifteen. Despite being far too young to embark upon Religious Life, Thérèse was a determined young woman and insisted her father take her to Rome to ask permission of the Pope!

Thérèse's obstinacy in getting her own way is amusing, but we must pity her poor widowed father, who was manipulated into giving his last precious daughter to the Church. What is far more inspiring, however, is Thérèse's 'Little Way', a deep but childlike spirituality of courage and kindness. Thérèse needed all the courage she could summon, because she contracted tuberculosis and died a long, drawn-out and distressing death at the age of twenty.

My most favourite 'call' story, however, is that of Gladys Aylward, the London parlour maid who fancied she was called to work in the Chinese missions. She was a contemporary of the famous Olympic runner, Eric Liddle, who refused to run on the Sabbath but got his gold medal in a race for which he had not trained. Eric left his beloved Scottish Highlands to work in China, and I calculate that he would have been in Shanghai when Gladys eventually arrived in China in the early twentieth century.

The story, as told in her biography, *The Small Woman*, is that Gladys applied to the Baptist Missionary Society to be trained for the Chinese Mission. The ministers, however, did not believe in her call and suggested she work as a servant or housekeeper for some retired elderly missionary. But Gladys was not deterred and she put a deposit on a ticket to China on the Trans-Siberian Railway. Just how many years it took her to earn the fare I am not sure, but eventually she set off with a small spirit stove and provisions for the journey. An obstacle arose when she arrived at Harbin in Mongolia, where there was a civil war raging. I can't remember how she travelled the last laps of her journey, save that she crossed to Japan and made her way north until she could take a boat to Shanghai. From there, she travelled hundreds of miles inland to seek out a Scottish missionary called Jeannie Lawson.

The two women worked together until Jeannie died, running an inn where they told Bible stories to the mule-drivers who stopped off with them en route to their destination. Their story is told (rather too sweetly for my taste) in the Ingrid Bergman film, *The Inn of the Sixth Happiness*. Some time after Jeannie died, China was in the turmoil of war and Gladys had to summon up all her courage to lead a group of more than one hundred small children to the safety of an orphanage run by Madame Chiang Kai-shek. The journey was over one hundred miles and the little band of refugees suffered all manner of privations, including being shot at from the air by the Japanese air force. After a month they arrived safely, but Gladys was completely exhausted and ill with both typhus and pneumonia. She died on 3 January 1970 in Taiwan, truly a valiant 'small woman'.

Stories like this inspire and intrigue me. What on earth put this crazy idea into Gladys's head? What gave her the courage to persevere until she had the money to travel and then to set out for such an unknown land? Was it the power of God? I believe it was.

I have recently learned another astonishing story, much closer to home. I worked for several years with a bright, rather unorthodox social worker called John Wright. John had breast cancer some time after me but soon returned to work, initially working with bereaved children but later with adults in a local community service. When I received news of his death from cancer earlier this year, I determined to go to his funeral in the nearby town of Totnes. The church was packed and, as I listened to the minister, I wondered if I had come to the wrong place, for he was talking about a John I had never met.

I pieced things together during the service and spoke to the pastor afterwards. John, I learned, had in the last five years of his life become a passionate Christian and evangelist. This witty, irreverent health-care professional had abandoned social work to spread the Word of God and had travelled to Africa, India and Europe with another missioner. He had settled eventually in Canada, marrying the daughter of the pastor with whom he was staying and eventually dying of terminal cancer in the local hospice. The ways of the Divine are indeed mysterious and greatly to be wondered at.

On a less pious note, since I retired and acquired my dogs, I have gradually become more open and approachable to strangers. Each day, morning and evening, Anka, Mollie and I solemnly walk the boundaries of Plymouth Hoe, a promontory overlooking our spectacular harbour. Our progress is slow, as many scents are to be investigated and messages left. Then, of course, there are other dogs to be interrogated and examined, so while this is going on I get to know the owners.

All this sounds mundane and not really the stuff of miracles, but I have met so many delightful people and made so many new friends that I see it as a very God-given experience. Perhaps I should explain that during my years as a hospital doctor I was very focused upon my patients and had no time for idle chat except with friends. What I have recently discovered is a new and surprising ability to be friendly to strangers and a delight in meeting all manner of people. Over the past five years I have met many delightful people whom I would have ignored completely in another era. There is a kind of etiquette for these meetings: one talks about the weather and asks the name of the stranger's dog. Then there is usually a small exchange of gifts (treats and biscuits) between myself and the stranger's dog, then between the stranger and my dogs. Eventually we run out of conversation and I mutter 'must get on' and call the dogs to heel; not that they come, you understand, because Chows are dogs of independent and stubborn disposition and come only when they are ready!

The first friends I met in this way were Frank and Charlie, two men in their sixties. Frank, with his head bald like an egg, is an ex-marine and father to Benjie and Feeny, two Lhasa Apsos – although in Charlie's time he also had a Doberman called Sadie. Charlie, alas, died of cancer a few years ago. He was *such* a lovely man, gentle and witty, and we miss him so much. The dogs still go the bench where he sat, hoping for a biscuit. Then there are Sandra and John, with their Cavalier King Charles Spaniel, Jamie. Always smartly dressed, Sandra is Welsh, a woman of sharp discernment and a wicked wit, with one of the kindest hearts I have known. I have co-opted her to work for our child bereavement charity, Jeremiah's Journey, so she is now both friend and colleague.

I realise that hearing about other people's dogs and neighbours is not to everyone's taste, so I will discipline myself not to tell you about Hugh, and his Bull Terrier, Bert (with whom Mollie is in love), nor Sadie, the wonderful chocolate-brown Newfoundland, nor Milo, the fabulous Alaskan Malamute. What I want to illustrate, however, is how a motley group of strangers somehow becomes formed into a community of friends simply by having the leisure and courage to admire each other's dogs.

Chapter 6

Finding God in Community

Unless we live together as brothers we shall perish together as fools.

Dr Martin Luther King Jr.

I write, as will be obvious to the discerning, by free association – one idea giving birth to a memory which, when explored, leads to another idea. I had not thought to write about community, largely because the word reminds me of convents and the unhappiness of those days, but I realise now that we all need friends and neighbours and that we, and these people, form a kind of community.

Our first experience of community is, of course, living as a member of a family group, and it is during the early years of life that we are formed as people. In the eight or so years that I have practised as a therapist, I have learned for myself how vital is the early experience of a loving, violence-free family community. Fighting between parents frightens a small child and damages his or her sense of security, as does emotional and physical abuse. The tragedy is that we learn our behaviours from our parents, so, if they are critical, denigratory or neglectful, we will believe this to be the norm and behave in a similar way. On the other hand, the healthy, stable environment of a loving, sharing home provides a precious legacy of good self-esteem and respect for others.

Our next experience of community is, of course, school, though, alas, not everyone finds this a nurturing experience; some mummy's little angel can be a cruel bully, given like-minded friends. A teacher who acts as mentor and confidante to a troubled child can, like a loving grandparent, provide a vital source of love and affirmation in the world of a young person with a dysfunctional family.

For me, community has always been in a hospital setting, in a group of people drawn together for a common and holy task. If reading medicine described as a *holy* task surprises you, think of Jesus the healer, the comforter and, of course, Jesus the worker of miracles. I have always loved hospitals since my days as a medical student, when my nose would twitch with excitement at the smell of ether (alas now replaced by no odour in particular). I know that hospitals receive a bad press these days, as we complain that they are dirty and there are not enough nurses to care for the sick, but even so, I still find an amazing selflessness in most doctors and nurses who struggle to diagnose, to heal and to comfort. I remember writing, rather piously, after I left the convent and returned to medicine: 'Hospital corridors are my cloister and I "tell" my patients as a nun "tells" her beads, gently and lovingly with a practised hand.' If you think I am getting a bit carried away, remember that we are talking about finding God in all things, and in hospitals God is to be found in the people; ordinary people, irreverent, sometimes immoral, but united in a single task – to heal the sick and mend the broken.

My most exciting experience of community, believe it or not, was in prison in Chile, crowded together with around eighty women whose language I understood but poorly. After three days in a torture centre and three weeks in solitary confinement, I was transferred to Tres Alamos (Three Poplars) prison, just outside of Santiago. The prison governor led me to a door, which he opened to reveal a sea of faces, young women, all eager to welcome the English doctor who had endured torture for treating one of their own.

The prison was built like a cloister, with rooms opening on to a rectangular yard where the girls walked and talked or sat at tables doing their craft work. Never before had so many people greeted me with such love and generosity. My hair kept getting in my eyes, so Anita Maria took the grip out of her own hair and quietly handed it to me. My need was greater than hers at that moment, so she went without that I might have what I needed. It was the same with food. All provisions brought by families were handed over to a common pool, from which they were redistributed so that all might have some or the sick have what they needed. I had been three weeks in solitary, living on a diet of thin soup and dry bread, and had lost a fair bit of weight (oh that I could do it so easily now!). This made me eligible for a daily helping of yoghurt, made by the girls from donations of milk powder from the Red Cross. Never had charitable donations been used so creatively nor distributed so fairly!

I have written before the story of my own lesson in sharing, but I will tell it again here for a new generation. In the week before Christmas, I was visited by Reggie Seconde, the British Ambassador, and his wife, who brought me not only a tin of Harrods sweets but a tinned Christmas cake. I was delighted: now I could repay my new friends' kindness, and, of course, impress them with the superior quality of English food. I should have known better. When I offered a sweet to Beatriz, who slept in the bunk above me, she was deeply shocked and said I should hand them in. I pleaded that twenty humbugs would not go far among the eighty of us, and, by dint of moral blackmail, persuaded her to have one. Poor Beatriz: my Christmas gift to her was a load of guilt which weighed her down and made her sad. At the time, I felt she was making an awful fuss, but I came to see later that she had broken her vow, her pledge to share all with the community.

It rapidly became clear that no one was going to share my precious cake with me, and I either had to hand it in or eat it all by myself in secret. With ill grace, therefore, I handed it over to the keeper of the food. I'm not quite sure just how I imagined they would share one small cake between eighty women, but I was completely unprepared to see it crumbled into an enormous bowl of manjar blanco – caramelised condensed milk – to make a dessert for us all. It wasn't exactly a loaves and fishes job but the nearest to it I've yet seen.

These were remarkable young women, and I have never met their like again. Mostly from the middle class, they were mainly university students or young professionals in social work, nursing or medicine. They came from comfortable homes but had, during the course of 'field work', been exposed to the appalling poverty of the rotos, the 'broken ones' who lived in shanty towns in 'houses' made literally of cardboard, sheet plastic and corrugated iron.

These women had all been delighted when the Socialist doctor, Salvador Allende, was elected as president of Chile in late 1971. They believed passionately (as did most of my Chilean friends) in Allende's peaceful revolution. Most of them had been politically active, which is how they came to be arrested, tortured and interned. I found them bright, intelligent and cheerful, though most carried a deep anger at the way they had been treated.

Most had been tortured and many raped but none treated as cruelly as two of the girls, Gladys Diaz and Nieves Ayres, captured in the early days after the coup of 1973.

Gladys was a journalist and senior member of the MIR, the revolutionary left. She had been tortured many, many times and held for some time in a cage, which was so small that she could neither stand nor lie. I met Gladys very briefly, just before I was released, and I will never forget her scorn when I said the Ambassador had advised me against speaking to the press. It was she who shamed me into telling the story of Chile's prisoners to anyone who would listen on my return to the UK. I feel sad now that Mr Seconde had given me the original advice, but no doubt he had my personal safety and wellbeing in mind.

Nieves Ayres, who was younger than Gladys, had also been picked up in the early days of the dictatorship, and imprisoned in the infamous Techas Verdes (Green Roofs) prison. It was there that the interrogators had a field day with the women prisoners, training a German Shepherd dog to rape them and putting rats in their vaginas. I have no evidence of this but it is what I was told and I believe it to be true.

How was it, then, that I found this community of socialists more loving than the nuns in the convent? Why did I feel more traumatised when I left the convent than when I was released from prison? Perhaps it is because I left Chile with a mission to fight for the release of my friends, while my departure from the convent felt only like failure. In hindsight, the prison community felt somehow more authentic, less studied, less aware of how it looked to those on the outside. I remember vividly being visited in the convent by a Benedictine friend, Father Brendan Smith, and being graciously allowed to take him coffee after lunch (though not to dine with him). I had just made two mugs of coffee to take to the 'parlour' when the Sister-in-charge of hospitality asked me what I was doing. When I told her I was taking coffee to Brendan, she exclaimed 'You can't give Father coffee in a mug!' and tipped the contents down the sink before making a pot of coffee for me to take. I know it's a small thing and she was only trying to be gracious, but I had a good long mutter about wasting food and trying to impress 'Father'.

How was it, then, that I found God – the Divine – more alive, more present, in a group of political prisoners than in a community of nuns? In hindsight, I can only say that the Chilean women were kinder, more generous, more open and more 'other-centred' than my sisters in the convent.

Beatriz, I recall, had a picture stuck to the wall beside her bed which somehow said it all: she had cut out the figure of a black child from a magazine, and placed it in the photograph of a beautiful living-room.

Beatriz wanted the poor to inherit the earth; I'm sure the nuns did too, but I guess it was less obvious to me.

There was, in Chile, a very small community by the sea which became my oasis for a couple of years. Run by two Maryknoll Sisters, it was designated a house of prayer and refreshment. One of the sisters was a great baker of cakes and I would chat to her when I arrived and then sit in the chapel and watch the sun go down over the sea. Most of my time was spent in silence, and I would sink into it as one does into a warm swimming pool. We rose before dawn and prayed together for three hours in silence: it seems a marathon now, but then it seemed only natural. Most of the time I spent face down on the chapel floor, a favourite position for prayer before my joints stiffened up for ever. Sometimes I fell asleep and they told me I snored gently – rather like my beloved black Chow, Mollie, who sleeps under my bed and snores from time to time. (During the holiday in which I write this chapter, I have received resigned text messages from Joanne, my wonderful dogsitter, saying that Mollie has kept her awake half the night. I delight in her complaint, which implies that she is too kind to do the logical thing: to boot Mollie out of the bedroom!)

It was in Chile that I returned to the practice of Catholicism after a 'lapse' of nearly ten years. It was after my doctor friend, Consuelo, died, and I had returned to the Church as if I'd never been away. Once a week, after being on night duty, I took the bus up to a Benedictine monastery in the hills, where I would spend the day in prayer – or at least gazing emptily at the mountains which came and went in the clouds, mist and city smog.

Although I never really got to know the monks, except the portero, Padre Angelo, who answered the door, I was grateful for their silent hospitality and the peace of their monastery.

As I write, it occurs to me that I am someone who likes to be on the edge of monastic communities but definitely not a member! I love to share in the liturgy, the sense of space and the God-talk, but I am too eccentric a person, too wild a spirit, to submit to any rule, discalced or shod. As I wrote earlier, the hospital is where I belong and its corridors are my cloister. Even the hospice was too confining, and I was always watching my back, so fearful of upsetting the matron or the governors that when I was sacked it was in some ways a relief. My crime (and I can understand their irritation) was being away lecturing too much, but the hospital which took me on accepted this as a part of who I was.

Thinking back, I ask myself if I found God in the hospice community? The answer, of course, is yes, but I think I found him/her in the patients, rather than in the peaceful atmosphere. In my experience, hospices are quite like convents in that they are inhabited by too many middle-aged women trying to be too perfect, a dynamic which leads inevitably to tensions and territorial conflicts.

There is an interesting book by Canadian nurse and psychologist Mary Vachon, Occupational Stress in the Care of the Dying, the Bereaved and the Critically Ill. During her research, Mary heard a familiar cry: 'It's not the patients who stress me, it's my colleagues!' I certainly found this to be true in the hospice community, and would marvel at the way visitors commented upon the wonderful atmosphere of love and peace when, behind the scenes, we were frequently to be found bitching about each other and our superiors.

It is the same with retreat houses: the peace so valued by the grateful retreatant is often bought at the cost of the inevitable tensions of community life.

It is just as well, I suppose, that I was thwarted in my ambition to found a community of monastic women based upon the little house of prayer run by the Maryknoll Sisters. My vision, and I still believe it to be valid, was of a group of women who would form a core monastic community, with recitation of the Divine Office (the psalms and scripture readings), manual and academic work and occasional sorties for preaching. The group would accept guests into its midst, to share its life for brief or longer stays. British readers will surely remember two television series, *The Monastery* and *The Monastery Revisited*, in which small groups of outsiders were welcomed into monastic communities for a period of four to six weeks. The impact upon the visitors and the community was fascinating to observe and, overall, extremely positive.

My blueprint, when it was dreamed up in the 1970s, was radical in that most (if not all) nuns would not admit visitors into their 'cloister', their personal space. Another issue in which my vision was at variance with the norm, was that 'my' nuns would not wear a religious habit, though they might have a uniform garment to put over their clothes for church services. I could write a whole chapter on how I hate religious habits, but that would divert us from the issue at hand. Suffice it to say, ordinary clothes would be worn.

I should add here that my vision, dreamed up in Chile, was very similar to one which came to fruition from Ampleforth Abbey in Yorkshire in the late 1970s, when three monks left the main community to begin a new venture on the outskirts of Liverpool – the community of Ince Benet (situated in Ince Blundell). One of the original monks left and another came but sadly died of a heart attack, leaving two men, one of whom had a great longing for the hermit life; this man, too, left, leaving only one monk, who has doggedly lived out his dream alone ever since. One of his chief aims was to live simply, in solidarity with the poor, and, amazingly, he has been totally faithful to this vision. We thanked God when he installed flush toilets but have been amazed to observe that life is possible in the twenty-first century without a fridge or a telephone, a mobile, a hi-fi or a computer!

Although no other monk has come to join him, there is a scattered 'community' of men and women who come to pray, to share in his life for a few days or to seek advice. Time was when I was a regular visitor, but now the distance and the demands of my canine friends make it too difficult. The truth is, perhaps, that I have found my own community of men, women and beasts, and no longer have to leave home in search of the Divine.

Chapter 7

Who are the Heathens Now?

When I was a child in primary school we saved our pennies to buy 'black babies'. If I remember rightly, we thought we were ransoming them, saving their souls by supporting the Missions, the groups of religious men and women who bravely left home and family to win the pagans for Christ. Ouch! This does not sound politically correct to our twenty-first century ears, for now we are people of inter-faith dialogue and we read the scriptures of other faiths: the Koran (perhaps), the Tao, the writings of the Buddha, or more likely their interpretation by Thich Nhat Hahn, and of course the poems of Rumi.

So what do we *really* think about other faiths and other religions? There is an old Catholic joke which goes something like this: Bill Bloggs dies and, on arriving at the gates of heaven, rings the bell. St Peter appears and says: 'Hello, Bill, welcome to heaven. Tell you what, I'm on my lunch break, so why don't I show you round a bit?' Bill is delighted, and off they go. They come to a cloud, from inside of which is issuing wonderful, loud band music. 'Who's there?' says Bill. 'Oh, it's the Salvation Army,' says St Peter. 'Ah yes,' says Bill, 'great musicians.' Then they pass another cloud and hear enthusiastic hymn singing. 'Who's in there?' says Bill. 'It's the Methodists,' says St Peter. 'Ah,' says Bill, 'wonderful singers.' Then, as they approach another cloud, St Peter whispers: 'Shush, don't say a word.' They tiptoe past and Bill, fascinated, says: 'So who's in there?' St Peter grins. 'It's the Catholics,' he says. 'They think they're the only people here!'

I've always loved this joke because it rings so true to my childhood experience. I really was taught that Christianity is the one true faith, and that Catholicism was somehow the best of all the Christian denominations. I remember clearly going to a non-Catholic wedding and being told to sit at the back and not join in the service, lest someone mistook me for a Protestant. The religious world, as I understood it then, was divided into Catholics and non-Catholics, whom we also referred to as Protestants, or 'Prots'. I had no idea that only a small percentage of non-Catholics were real Protestants, or that the latter were a proud group of men and women who thought even less of the Roman Catholics than we did of them!

I have a good friend, John, whose family comes from Northern Ireland, and every now and then it slips out how much he has been brought up to hate and despise the Church of Rome.

This animosity and distrust between Catholics and Protestants lies just beneath the surface amongst many Irish Christians, despite the cessation of 'the Troubles' that caused so much bloodshed in Northern Ireland. Far greater, of course, after 9/11, is the distrust between Christians (practising and nominal) and Muslims. I have to admit with both shame and embarrassment to a completely irrational dislike of the veil used by some Muslim women, especially the one that covers their faces. I look at them in the street and think: 'Why do you have to be so different from us? Why can't you wear western clothes and let the wind ruffle your hair?' It's not that I challenge Islam as such, because I know that they believe in the same God as I, but their determination to be different narks me. How easy it is to cling to our own tribal gods and throw stones at those of others.

We are so lucky to live in this time of greater openness to those with a faith different to our own. The scriptures of other religions have been translated for us, and we meet our own God face-to-face in snatches from the Koran or the Tao. The television, too, is an amazing source of education about the different faiths – that is, if we choose the religious documentaries over comedy and cooking!

One of the things that helps me to understand a number of different faiths is the fact that I am deeply theocentric in my worship, rather than Christocentric. What I mean by this is that my instinct is to pray to the unknown, mysterious God – what the early Jews called El Shaddai, the God of the Mountain. This means that I am at home in any monotheistic faith because I believe we are all worshipping the unknown, mysterious creator of the Universe.

Many Christians, on the other hand, are deeply Christocentric, in that they find the Divine most available and attractive in the figure of Jesus in the Gospels, or in the risen Christ. Many Christians, in fact seem to use the words God, Jesus and Christ interchangeably. I remember that one of my fellow novices in the convent used to describe changing the tabernacle veil as 'changing Jesus' jumper! She did not, of course, mean to be disrespectful nor did she really think that Jesus of Nazareth was present in the received sacrament. So, what *did* she mean? Did she mean that God the Father was in the Host, or in the Risen Christ or the Holy Spirit? Trinitarian theology is hard enough to understand without confusing all three persons in the one God with the man Jesus.

I can't say I find the concept of the Trinity particularly helpful, probably because I encompass all three 'members' under the word God or the Divine. I love, however, the images used in poetry: Hopkins' 'Holy Ghost' who broods over our world with 'warm breast and with ah! bright wings,' (Gerard Manley Hopkins, 'God's Grandeur'), and Thompson's 'and lo, Christ walking on the water, not of Genesareth but Thames' (Francis Thompson, 'No Strange Land').

As I wrote earlier, I personally am more at home with the El Shaddai of the early desert worshippers, or Yahweh, whose face cannot be seen or his name uttered out loud. This (not those) is my God transcendent, but *also* my God immanent. I would claim to have a personal relationship with the Divine whom I *experience* as both immanent and transcendent.

Jesus I understand as the *man* who lived and died in Palestine and rose from the dead to *become* the Christ, the Immortal Son of God, who is somehow at the heart of our Universe. Already I feel confused, but does it really matter? My faith in the Divine is sufficiently robust to withstand the multiple use and understanding of the Divine Names: Wonderful Counsellor, Mighty God, Eternal Father, Prince of Peace, along with Allah and the Tao, who are all, for me, like facets of the same diamond, the mystery which we call God.

> For there is a child born for us, a son given to us,
> and dominion is laid on his shoulders;
> And this is the name they give him:
> Wonderful, Counsellor, Mighty God,
> Eternal Father, Prince of Peace.
>
> Isaiah 9:6

My hunch is that it is more difficult for someone whose devotion is to Jesus to feel at home with the divinities of other religions. If Jesus is my brother and my friend, how can I feel at home with Allah (his name be praised) or the Prophet (peace be upon him)? It is so hard for people to reconcile a monotheistic theology which talks of a mysterious, all-loving, creator God with a doctrine which condemns homosexuals and women who break their marriage vows, and which cuts off the right hand of the thief. We Christians think of such teaching as completely barbaric, while neatly forgetting about the Spanish Inquisition and the martyrdom of Protestants.

We forget, however, that the teachings of Islam have been corrupted over the centuries, in the same way that the Christian doctrines have been misunderstood and twisted to fit in with someone's world view.

I have found it enormously interesting and mind-stretching to visit a number of very different cultures. Bali, in particular, springs to mind with its numerous beautiful temples and gentle people. My religious teacher in primary school would surely have classed them as pagans, but now that I know something of Buddhism, I feel only empathy for their tradition of offerings and processions.

I remember, too, sitting on the beach in Rio, watching people toss flowers into the sea and leave bread and champagne on the beach for their departed loved ones. How very human their worship: so like the flowers we left on the roadside when my nephew Peter and his son, Sam, were killed in a motorbike accident a few years ago.

In my work with Jeremiah's Journey, our programme for bereaved children, I work with the adult groups and have recently been very struck by how the bereaved cling to the physical remains of those who have died. One couple who lost a baby have visited the grave daily for three years. In Christian terms, there is nothing there but a collection of bones, and the soul of the baby is with God; but that's not the parents' experience. In their anguish, they return constantly to the last place they saw 'Tammy', hoping against hope to find some vestige of his presence.

Even more precious are the ashes of those who have been cremated. One family passed the urn containing their lost child's ashes to whoever in the family needed comfort, and another mother put a portion of her daughter's ashes in a teddy bear, so she could cuddle her when she felt distressed. Who am I to say this is crazy, that it makes no sense in religious terms? This is what people do: this is *their* religion, their mourning ritual, and we can only respect it while acknowledging that it is not *our* way.

Different people in different cultures all have their own ways of interceding with the Gods. We Catholics pray to the saints, to Mary and to God; Hindus make little offerings of fruit, flowers and cake. The Jews used to slaughter the best lamb in their flock, or a pair of turtledoves, and burn them as an offering to Yahweh. Today's modern pagans have lucky charms or objects, hardly more advanced than primitive African tribes. One man's religious nutter is another's Shaman or holy man, so surely it behoves us to respect each other's beliefs and rituals? 'True,' I hear you say, '*but* …'

… *But* what about religions which lead to people hurting themselves or others? What do we think of the suicide bomber, or of the practice of female circumcision? Should we accept the stoning of adulterous women, and the amputating of the thief's hand? Do we know enough of Sharia Islamic Law to welcome it in Britain? I know nothing of this latter issue but am deeply against violent mutilating punishments and the death penalty, while suicide bombing I find an abomination. But does believing another's religious practice to be wrong entitle us to interfere with it? Should we rescue the victim if we can, or gently educate our brothers that what they are doing is wrong?

I'm not sure this is getting me any closer to the truth, but it *does* help me to understand why the Christian missionaries gave their lives to changing what they believed to be wrong. My experience of missionary nuns and priests in Chile was an enormously positive one. The days of imposing our religion and liturgy on a group of hapless native people have long gone. Inculturation, the adapting of Christian practices to the host society, is now mandatory in Catholic missionary practice.

My American Sister and priest friends in Chile risked their lives to help Marxist men and women hide from the secret police, whilst two of my closest friends died while helping people on the run. Ita Ford and Carla Piette were two Maryknoll Sisters who had been in Chile for over twenty years. In 1979, they volunteered to work in El Salvador where there was a pressing need for volunteers to work with the orphans of civil war. One night, Ita and Carla offered to take a man home because he was scared of being recognised where he was. It was a night of torrential rain and when they had dropped the man off, the Sisters had to cross a river in flood. They had crossed it safely earlier, but now the force of the water over-turned their jeep and they were each carried down the river. Ita managed to make it to safety, but Carla's body was found at daybreak, naked and battered, miles down the river.

It took Ita a long time to recover from the trauma of that night and the loss of her friend, but in December of 1980, she returned from a community meeting in Nicaragua with renewed commitment to the work in El Salvador. She and Sister Maura Clarke, also of Maryknoll, were met by work colleagues Jeannie Donovan, a lay missioner, and Dorothy Kazel, an Ursuline Sister. The four women set off for home, but were intercepted by the military. Their bodies were found in a shallow grave on the mountainside several days later. They had been raped then shot through the head.

Why, why such violence, such bestiality? We knew only that the order came from higher up in the chain of command and that they were killed because they were seen as a threat to the regime. Four women who looked after orphans, a threat to the State? It's hard to understand.

The life of Jeannie Donovan is especially interesting and has been told both in a book, called *Roses in December*, and a film of the same name (the film used to be available for hire from CAFOD, the Catholic Fund for Overseas Development). Jeannie was an American student who went on a high school exchange to Cork, where she met a priest who had worked in Latin America. His description of poverty and injustice never left her and after a few years sowing her wild oats, she gave up a highly-paid job to work for the Philadelphia Lay Missionary Programme in Latin America. She too worked with orphans and became so committed that she extended her stay. The film shows moving footage of her on holiday with her fiancé; she was neither a nun nor a plaster saint. On being asked why she was returning to El Salvador after R and R in the States, she said something like: 'It's children, the children, how could I leave them?' Then she added, with a smile: 'After all, where else could you find roses in December?'

'Thou shalt not have false gods before Me,' it says in the Ten Commandments, and we Christians have always assumed God meant Baal, and all the other pagan deities men have worshipped since time began. It probably never occurs to most of us that it is all too easy to be a Christian *and* worship false gods. It's too easy to say that money and sex and power are the false gods of our time, but it's also too easy to dismiss the saying. Power in particular can seduce men and women into all kinds of corrupt behaviour, as can fear of the loss of property and a comfortable lifestyle. The example I know best is of the way the CIA supported the Pinochet regime during the overthrow of the Socialist government of Chile's democratically-elected president, Doctor Salvador Allende. The financial assistance amounted to some eight million dollars. While my friends and I were queuing for flour, oil and toilet paper in August 1973, America was bankrolling the long drivers' strike, which brought about the food shortages which eventually brought down the Allende regime.

Ever fearful of the rising tide of Communism in its own backyard (South America), the Americans have spent millions supporting the status quo, in which around ninety-five per cent of the land and wealth of countries like Guatemala, Chile, Salvador and Nicaragua remains in the hands of the wealthy five per cent of the population. I have vivid memories of a weekend spent in the South of Chile with my plastic surgeon boss. We were served a meal of several courses by waiters in white gloves, and the napkins were whisked away after every course and replaced with fresh ones of impeccably-starched linen. Doctor Raphael Ursua had a private island which he stocked with deer for American businessmen to come and shoot. That, for me, is worship of the idol of a luxurious lifestyle.

That, of course, was then, and we are now entering a period of recession. Even so, idol worship is all around us: worship of the body beautiful, of the fast car, of the luxurious house, and, of course, of the delicious meal. I have just read *Acqua Alta*, a novel by Donna Leon, whose policeman Guido Brunetti tracks down the elusive criminals of Venice. The villain, de Capra, is a ruthless millionaire with a passion for rare and beautiful artefacts, especially Chinese ceramics. He kills and kills again, just to obtain priceless prehistoric pottery and ancient jade to adorn his private and secret gallery. *That* is true twenty-first century idolatry.

One of the factors that makes it so difficult for us to know if we are pagans is the fact that our idols are often good and beautiful. It is right and proper for us to take care of our bodies, to exercise and eat healthy food. There is nothing holy in living in an uncomfortable house with ugly artefacts; the urge to create a beautiful and welcoming home is so instinctive for some women that it must be 'hard wired' in the brain. The difficulty I have is knowing when to stop! Like many women, I love shopping and furnishing my house with beautiful and colourful things is an ongoing delight. One of the reasons I hated the convent was its lack of colour and beauty. I have, though, over the years, worked out what I hope is a balance between greed and restraint. Because asceticism is not really my thing, I try to share my possessions with my friends and give away my excesses. I keep today's purchase and lend or give away yesterday's.

I love, too, to cook and entertain friends and colleagues once or twice a week. When they have departed I feast upon what is left for days and then give the leftovers of the leftovers to the dogs. Mostly I try, but often fail, to follow Mahatma Gandhi's maxim:

'Live simply that others may simply live.'

As my bank balance travels inexorably into the red zone, I dismiss my occasional urges to cancel standing orders to Oxfam, Save the Children, Amnesty, *Médecins Sans Frontières,* and so on. It's an untidy system, but it works, although sometimes I daren't use my debit card and there is no money in the jar. Having said that, there's always enough to pay for a cappuccino by the sea. We all have our priorities!

Chapter 8

Now: Where is Your God?

Today is 11 September, or 'nine-eleven' – 9/11, as the Americans like to call it. Today I was going to write about St Paul, but somehow I have no heart for it: my mind is full of sadness, anger and bewilderment as I am reminded of the horror of that day in 2001.

So where was love on 11 September 2001, and where was God? Had he gone to sleep on the sofa or turned his mobile off? Before I struggle with these questions and pit my puny wits against the Goliath of 'the problem of evil', I need to put in a word for Chile, my adopted Latin American country. On 11 September 1973, the democratically-elected government of Doctor Salvador Allende was overthrown by a military coup. For the Chileans 9/11 was the end of over one hundred years of democracy and the beginning of a fifteen-year nightmare of cruel dictatorship in which torture, disappearance and death became daily occurrences. Bloated bodies floated down the Mapocho river, which runs through the centre of Santiago; men and women were dropped to their death in the sea from helicopters, their hands bound behind their backs with barbed wire. Hundreds were held in prison camps, from Dawson Island in the cold south to the desert town of Antofagasta in the north. Don't tell me that this is communist propaganda, because I was there. I saw the trucks full of armed soldiers pass my house and I was a prisoner not just in Santiago's Tres Alamos and Cuatro Alamos detention centres, but also in the notorious Villa Grimaldi, where I and men and women like me were tortured until they broke or died.

All this was over thirty-five years ago, almost forgotten by one generation, but vividly remembered by those of us who were there. Now, of course, there is the American 9/11, that terrible day when Muslim extremists hijacked several passenger aircraft and flew two of them straight into the Twin Towers, the two tallest skyscrapers in the heart of Manhattan.

I've often wondered why the terrorists chose the same date as the Chilean military to unleash their 'dogs of war'. Is there some dark significance? Were they punishing the USA for its complicity in the overthrow of Allende, or was it just a bizarre coincidence? Whatever the answer, America has unwittingly hijacked Chile's memorial day for its own.

My real question here concerns both tragedies equally: where was God when the Moneda (the Chilean House of Government in downtown Santiago) was bombed, and where was she when the Twin Towers crumbled like a child's pile of bricks? I can tell you where I was on both occasions: in 1973, I was in the open market buying food for my household. The planes flew loudly overhead and then, to our astonishment, dropped bombs on the city centre. People cried out in fear and horror and ran for their homes. I filled my basket with greens from a deserted stall and hurried back to my house to find my friends listening to the radio, from which a harsh voice proclaimed that there had been a military coup and that certain people were to present themselves to the police. A further announcement informed us that there was *toque de queda total* – a total curfew – until further notice. That night, shots rang out near our house and a helicopter without lights circled menacingly over the city and its frightened people.

In 2001, I was teaching at St Luke's Hospice in Plymouth and came out of a lecture to see the demolition of the Twin Towers on the television. The sight was mesmerising! We stared in disbelief as the plane flew straight into the first tower and then, some minutes later, as the skyscraper disintegrated before our eyes. It was so far away, so unreal, that I was fascinated and appalled but not really moved at the time. Later, of course, we learned the true human cost of this enterprise: the three thousand dead, and many so crushed that their bodies were never found.

When the initial horror and drama had passed, we law-abiding people asked: 'Why?' Why had *they* done it? Why did *they* hate 'us', the ordinary westerners, so much? To us, the notion of suicide bombing, of making a holocaust of one's life to kill the enemy, is incomprehensible. Yes, we sent and still send thousands of young men and women to risk their lives on the battlefield, but to deliberately kill oneself that others might die seems to us somehow obscene.

By the time this book is published, all this will be more than nine years ago and, as time passes, we learn more and more about these rather alien young men and women who feel 'called' to wage 'Jihad' against us. During the course of the past few weeks, as I write, there has been much metaphorical searching in the rubble of the Twin Towers. We have 'met' (by television interview) several of the families who lost relatives that day. They told us how they worked alongside the fire fighters, desperately hoping that their son or brother or friend was still alive. The fire fighters themselves worked tirelessly, searching underground in rooms which had descended almost intact to form a subterranean grave. They thought they would find people wounded, trapped, alive; but they were wrong. In the act of falling, the building acted like some hideous, giant centrifuge and everyone was killed.

They, the terrorists, did it to strike a political and psychological blow against the United States: but why? The answer, we are told by other young men in their farewell videos before they too go off to die, is because of the aggressive foreign policies of the West against the Muslim world; it is because their 'brother Muslims' in Palestine are suffering at the hands of the Jews; and subsequent terror attacks are also because of the way the West has invaded Iraq and Afghanistan. They despise us too, because of our way of life; they find our young men and women indecent in their dress and immoral in their behaviour. In particular, they are scornful about the way we, and especially our young people, drink. All of this they see as an abomination; an insult to them and to their God.

How unbelievably sad and complex it all is. The Americans helped the Chileans overthrow Allende because they were afraid of Latin America 'going communist'. The Chilean upper and middle classes supported Pinochet because they were afraid that Allende would take away their land and their houses. And the British and the Americans invaded Iraq because they were convinced that the Iraqis had weapons of mass destruction – atomic weapons which they would use to destroy our civilisation. As it turned out, there were no such weapons and the scientist who had searched and found nothing took his own life after his advice was ignored.

I find this story so very sad because so much of the evil done has been committed in good faith by good men and women. I don't believe our leaders are evil people: they may be misguided, blind or arrogant, but they are not evil. Likewise, the people we fight and kill are not evil. They too are doing what they believe to be right.

It is so easy to hate the young terrorists as they rant against us, but they too are sons and daughters, mothers and fathers, pursuing what they see as a call from God. We have to make our own the maxim that one should hate the sin and love the sinner. The tragedy, of course, is that we are *all* sinners: misguided, ill-informed, bigoted and blind. We think that *we* are God's people and those we oppose are Satan's; and they think the same of us.

G. K. Chesterton puts it better than I can in his 'A Hymn for the Church Militant':

> Great God, that bowest sky and star,
> Bow down our towering thoughts to thee,
> And grant us in a faltering war
> The firm feet of humility.
>
> Lord, we that snatch the swords of flame,
> Lord, we that cry about Thy ear,
> We too are weak with pride and shame,
> We too are as our foemen are.
>
> Yea, we are mad as they are mad,
> Yea we are blind as they are blind,
> Yea, we are very sick and sad
> Who bring good news to all mankind?

So where is God in all this? Is she wringing her hands in heaven like an impotent parent while her children fight? Perhaps: I am certain she weeps for us all. More importantly, God is immanent, in us and with us: present equally in killer and killed, in the Afghan rebel as he fashions his roadside bomb and in the British father of three who is blown to bits when he treads on it somewhere down south in Helmand Province.

This concept of God suffering in and with us is a hard one to grasp; yet it reoccurs frequently in spiritual writings of different faiths. In *Night*, Elie Wiesel's account of his time in Auschwitz, he tells the story of the execution by hanging of a child:

> One day, when we came back from work, we saw three gallows rearing up in the assembly place, three black crows ... Three victims in chains – and one of them the little servant, the 'sad eyed angel'.

Two men and the boy were hanged but the child took a long time to die –
perhaps because he weighed so little.

> For more than half an hour he stayed there, struggling between
> life and death, dying in slow agony under our eyes.

Behind him, Elie heard for the second time a man ask:

> 'Where is God now?' And I heard a voice within me answer him
> 'where is He? Here He is – He is hanging here on these gallows.'
>
> … That night the soup tasted of corpses.

Perhaps this is why Jesus had to die the way he did; he had to be in
solidarity with us, to suffer as humankind must suffer at each other's
hands. After all, if he'd died a peaceful death we'd doubt that he could
ever understand us; as it is, there is little that we experience that he has
not shared.

The notion that God suffers in and with us is one thing, but a theology
that puts God in the heart of the raping pirate or the Nazi executioner is
something else. And yet it seems to rise up intuitively in the minds of very
different people. Thich Nhat Hanh, whom I quoted earlier, was not
always a pious monk but a human rights protester on the streets of war
torn Hanoi in Vietnam. How curious then that he should echo the
thoughts of the English Christian mystic, Caryll Houselander, writing
during the Second World War.

In *A Rocking-horse Catholic*, Houselander relates a vision, or rather an
insight, which occurred to her while on a crowded underground train in
the London rush hour:

> Quite suddenly I saw with my mind, but as vividly as a
> wonderful picture, Christ in them all.

She goes on to recount not only her sense of Christ living and dying,
rejoicing and sorrowing in these people, but of all humanity, past,
present and to come, being there. It is her insight about 'sinners', however, which is relevant to my theme:

> I saw too, the reverence that everyone must have for a sinner;
> instead of condoning his sin, which is in reality his utmost
> sorrow, one must comfort Christ who is suffering in him.

She continues:

> And this reverence must be paid even to those sinners whose souls seem to be dead, because it is Christ who is the life of the soul who is dead in them: they are his tombs, and Christ in the tomb is potentially the Risen Christ. For the same reason, no one of us who has fallen into mortal sin himself must ever lose hope ...

Lecturing in London recently, about my Chile experience, I was asked, as I so often am, whether I felt able to forgive my torturers. I explained again that I had known from the outset that the men who tortured me were merely pawns, men used by others to extract information or control their 'enemies'. The men I held responsible were those who order the torture, both in Chile and in the far away USA. Sick, sadistic men and women may enjoy inflicting pain but it is those who manipulate people from afar who are ultimately, truly, culpable.

And yet, even they are sick; warped, narcissistic, greedy and cruel, and I can believe that they are the foetid tombs of the dead Christ. And because Christ rose from the dead, I can believe that these men too can be redeemed. It is in no way beyond the power of the Divine to change these men, however evil. This is why we must never despair; always hope for change, for conversion, for redemption.

Part III

Finding God in the Written Word

Wait for the riven
Word. It will be spoken,
It will be heard. It is
The time for speech, the
Bursting wide of flesh.
Like golden juice from the
Ripened peach, it will
Spill, it will pour, it will
Run down your famished face.

Feast your lips on this
Food. Fill your mouth with this
Fruit. Feed your soul on this
Fat. It is good. It is God.
It is food of life, the
Fountain of speech,
The word that satisfies.

O come and eat.
O taste and see:
How good a feast. How rich a
Guest. How lavish a host.
How ravished a hunger.
I am meet. I am meat.
I am ate. I am full. I am fed.
I am juice, I am joy, I am golden
Peach. I am flesh of your
Flesh, bone of my own solid
Bone. I am word. I am
Spoken. I am food. I am

Eaten. I am incarnate, Holy Bread.
I am born.
I am come. I am home.

Nicola Slee

Chapter 9

Finding God in the Old Testament

The word of God is alive and active.
Hebrews 4:12

The thing about finding God in the Old Testament is that you have to
know where to look; you need a guide, preferably a human one, who is so
besotted with the scriptures that he or she will set you on fire with
excitement. My guide was Father Bonaventure, a monk from Ampleforth, who taught me to navigate by means of the cross-references
alongside the text in the annotated Jerusalem Bible. In this particular
edition of the Bible it is possible to explore the great *themes* of the
scriptures, such as Glory or Kingdom or Love; this method involves
choosing a particular text, reading it and then looking at the references
alongside it. You then put in a marker where you are and turn to the
passages listed in the reference. You repeat the process and follow where it
leads you: into lots of other books in both the Old and New Testaments
including, of course, the various letters of St Paul, St John and the others.
It is enormous fun and deeply rewarding, like a treasure hunt or a search
for hidden Easter Eggs.

When I look back to my time at Ampleforth, and in the convent, I am
sure it was for this reason: that I should become familiar with the
scriptures. Or, to put it more accurately, that I should become familiar
with certain key passages in the scriptures, especially the words of the
prophets, who castigated the people for their wrongdoing and foretold
the coming of the Messiah. I have to admit right away that I am not at all
familiar either with the various battles that provided the backdrop to
these prophecies or with the image of an angry God with a long white

beard. The God I find in the Old Testament is the mysterious Yahweh, who loves his people with a passion that is hard for us to comprehend. In the brief space of this chapter I hope to introduce the reader to some of my favourite passages. The rest is up to you.

Beginning at the beginning, in the book of Genesis we have the Creation story, and the wonderful words:

> God saw all that he had made, and indeed it was very good.
>
> Genesis 1:31

I have neither time nor inclination to debate the notion that Genesis 1 and 2 are a factual description of the way our world came about. As a scientist of sorts, I am totally convinced by the theory of evolution and see it as God's way of creating the Universe.

There is, however, a passage which troubles me:

> God said, 'Let us make man in our own image, in the likeness of ourselves, and let them be masters of the fish of the sea, the birds of heaven, the cattle, all the wild animals and all the creatures that creep along the ground.'
>
> Genesis 1:26

What did he mean by 'master'? Did he mean we should subdue the animals and use them for our own purposes, or were we meant to cherish them as fellow creatures? More of this in Chapter 18. My favourite passage in Genesis is the story of the call of Abraham:

> Yahweh said to Abraham, 'leave your country, your family and your Father's House, for the land I will show you.'
>
> Genesis 12:1

Listen carefully: God did not say 'Go to Africa, China or the East Indies!' No; he did not commit himself. He assumed that Abraham would trust him and that he would set off into the unknown in blind faith. This is the first *call* story and it is our story too, for we are all called by name, into the unknown, for a particular mission of the Divine. We can dream about our future all we like but we must trust in God that he will not ask of us more than we can give.

One of the most exciting of the biblical call stories is the tale of Moses, the Hebrew child found by Pharaoh's daughter hidden in the bulrushes.

Despite his misgivings, Pharaoh allowed his daughter to arrange care for the foundling and Moses grew up in the court to be a rich and powerful young man. One day, the story goes, Moses came upon an Egyptian beating up a Hebrew slave. Furious, he killed the Egyptian and, after burying him in the sand, went about his business. Next day, however, he found two Hebrews fighting and, when he remonstrated with them, one of them said: 'Who appointed *you* to be a prince over us and judge? Do you intend to kill me as you killed the Egyptian?' Realising that all was known, Moses fled for the land of Midian, which lies to the east of the Gulf of Aqaba. As ever, he landed on his feet and married the daughter of a local herdsman, expecting to live happily ever after (Exodus 2:11–22). However, he had not bargained for Yahweh, the God of Sinai, taking an interest in him.

Time passed and the King of Egypt died, but the Sons of Israel, the captive Hebrews, were still groaning in their slavery and beseeching God to rescue them. It is at this point, so the Bible tells us, that Yahweh remembered his covenant with Abraham, Isaac and Jacob: the promise to be with them always, to increase their numbers and make them 'most fruitful'. You can read the covenant passages in the Book of Genesis, as I did with my tutor, and understand that Yahweh is *our* God too: that he calls us by name, promises to be with us and make us bear much fruit.

Moses' call came to him in the wilderness as he was looking after his father-in-law's flock. It is here that we find the famous story of the burning bush. As Moses neared Horeb, the mountain of God, an angel of the lord appeared to him 'in the shape of a flame of fire, coming from the middle of a bush'. Marvelling at the sight, and not a little nervous, Moses approached the fire and was amazed to find that the bush was not burnt up. 'Moses, Moses,' said the voice of Yahweh from its centre, 'Come no nearer … Take off your shoes for the place on which you stand is holy ground. I am the God of your father, the God of Abraham, the God of Isaac and the God of Jacob' (Exodus 3:1–6).

Yahweh told the terrified Moses, who by now had covered his face with his cloak, that he had a mission for him. 'I have seen the miserable state of my people in Egypt,' God said, and then: 'I send you to Pharoah to rescue them.'

My guess is that there have been many 'Moses' since those days; ordinary people going about their business, who have seen their own version of a burning bush and 'heard' the Lord's voice sending them on a mission.

I don't mean that we 'hear' the Lord's voice with our ears, but that suddenly, or gradually, we understand what we have to do, the path we have to follow. For Gladys Aylward, it was China, and trekking hundreds of miles with a bunch of hungry, frightened kids. For me, it was medicine, Chile and prison; for my friends Ita and Carla, it was El Slavador and martyrdom. We know not the day nor the hour, only that our God, who is also the God of all people, will be 'with us', just as I knew him there while I was being tortured.

I think that this concept of an all-powerful, all-loving God who calls us by name into the unknown is a really important one to grasp because it answers the inevitable human wail: 'Why me?' 'Why have I got cancer?' 'Why must my child die?' These are such poignant, human questions that we long to have them answered; but the only answer is: 'Why not?' The fact that cyclones and tsunamis wipe out thousands does not prove that there is *no* God, only that we do not understand the ways of the Divine. We confuse the concept of an all-powerful creator God with a God who intervenes in our world. Does God intervene? How can you or I know? What I do know is that belief in God makes me ask for help. The absurd thing is that I can, intellectually, have a fairly sophisticated theology of a Divine Creator, while at the same time asking God to find me a parking space. I know it's crazy, but humankind has been turning to its gods since time began. My atheist friends would say: 'In the beginning, man/woman created God.' Maybe; who knows? All I know is that my beliefs make sense and my faith sustains me – in the good times and the bad.

For me, the most exciting parts of the Old Testament are the meetings between different individuals and the Divine. The book of Exodus is particularly rich in descriptions of Moses' meetings with Yahweh. The account of the delivery of the stone tablets on which were written the Ten Commandments is wonderfully mysterious and dramatic. The Lord ordered Moses to come to him on the mountain and, trembling, Moses obeyed:

> The cloud covered the mountain, and the glory of Yahweh settled on the mountain of Sinai; for six days the cloud covered it, and on the seventh day Yahweh called to Moses from inside the cloud.
>
> Exodus 24:15–16

What are we to make of this story? Is it literally true or is the writer trying to convey Moses' wonder and awe at his experience of the Divine? When

Moses came down from the mountain after forty days and forty nights, we are told that, 'his face shone and the people were afraid of him' (Exodus 34:29–30).

In these encounters we have a wonderful image of the friendship that is possible between the human and the Divine. This is not a stroll along the road to Emmaus with the risen Christ, but a glimpse of the 'Glory', an awesome experience that makes individuals fling themselves on the ground in a terror, which is mysteriously joyous at the same time.

When the going got tough and the people were rebelling, Moses begged God to reveal the divine splendour once more. This time God spelt it out to Moses: 'You cannot see my face, for a man cannot see me and live.' Then came a revelation of the extraordinary tenderness of the Lord:

> I will put you in a cleft of the rock and shield you with my hand while I pass by. Then I will take my hand away and you shall see the back of me; but my face is not to be seen.
>
> Exodus 33:18–24

Irina Ratushinskaya, the Russian poet imprisoned by the KGB in Siberia, glimpses God's 'back parts' in a frosted prison window:

> And I will tell of the first beauty
> I saw in captivity.
> A frost covered window! No spy holes, nor walls,
> Nor cell bars, nor the long endured pain –
> Only a blue radiance on a tiny pane of glass …
> 'I Will Love and Survive' in *No, I'm Not Afraid*

'Such a gift, she writes, 'can only be received once. And perhaps is only needed once.'

This glimpse of the elusive Divine comes to us in different ways but the impact is always the same: a mixture of awe and wonder and unutterable joy. But God does not bestow these visions of 'Glory' lightly: there is always a reason, be it a call to serve, or affirmation of a course of action already taken.

The call of the prophet Isaiah is another *theophany*: a showing forth of God's glory. Isaiah had a vision of the Divine which was much more exotic than that of Moses. He saw God seated on a throne in the sanctuary, surrounded by six winged seraphs who cried out to one another: 'Holy, Holy, Holy is Yahweh Sabaoth.' The foundations of the threshold shook with the voice of the one who cried out, and the Temple was filled with smoke.

Isaiah was spooked out of his mind, and said:

> What a wretched state I am in! I am lost,
> For I am a man of unclean lips
> And I live among a people of unclean lips,
> And my eyes have looked at the King, Yahweh Sabaoth.
> Isaiah 6:1–5

Here we are reminded of the pleas of Moses: 'Lord, I am no good to you; I stutter; don't choose me! Take my brother, my friend, anyone but me!' But God paid scant attention to Isaiah's protestations, sending an angel with a live coal from the altar to cleanse his life. His defences removed, Isaiah heard the words that would change his life:

> 'Whom shall I send? Who will be our messenger?'

Isaiah could not resist and, like Mary, he said 'Yes':

> I answered, 'Here I am, send me'.
> Isaiah 6:8

I am always enormously moved by the simplicity of these words, 'Here I am'. 'I'm stupid and greedy and sinful, but, Lord, if I'm any good to you, take me, I'm yours'; this is my prayer, and yours: the prayer of any mortal, scared, but willing to be used for the Lord's purposes.

There are so many more wonderful passages of Isaiah that I could quote, but I shall content myself with the one that Jesus chose when he began his preaching mission. We are told that he went to the temple and, taking the scroll of the prophet Isaiah, proclaimed his calling:

> The spirit of the Lord has been given to me,
> For he has anointed me.
> He has sent me to bring the good news to the poor,
> (To heal the broken hearted,)
> To proclaim liberty to captives
> And to the blind new sight,
> To set the downtrodden free,
> To proclaim the Lord's year of favour.
> Luke 4:18–19 (quoting Isaiah 61:1, 8)

Some alternative translations have more poetic phrases: 'new sight to the blind' comes from the quoting of Isaiah in Luke 5, while 'to set the downtrodden free' comes from the hymn based on this passage.

I believe that, as Christians, we cannot exaggerate the importance of these two passages, Isaiah 61 and Luke 4:18–19, for they state so clearly that, when Jesus began his ministry, he chose a passage on what we now call 'social justice' to explain his mission. He did not quote from the passages which define how liturgy should be performed, nor did he say he would purge the church of prostitutes and homosexuals. No. He chose this passage of Isaiah, which expresses a call to care for the poor, the lonely, the imprisoned and the downtrodden. *This*, for me, is the essence of Christianity, and I wonder how it is that we so often forget this central message and become obsessed by peripheral issues.

After Isaiah came the prophet Jeremiah, another man called by name to proclaim God's word. Jeremiah has somehow acquired a reputation as a prophet of doom, but my favourite passage from this book is full of hope. In Jeremiah 18, we find the lovely story of God as a potter, forming his people with loving hands on the wheel.

In case you've never tried to make a clay pot, I should explain that you take a lump of clay and mould it with your hands on a moving wheel. 'Throwing' a pot is very much an acquired art, and the beginner will produce many misshapen vessels before he or she can make an acceptable pot. The great thing, however, is that clay can be re-cycled and reformed so the most misshapen vessel can be reshaped into a thing of beauty.

This is how Yahweh came to explain his power to Jeremiah: 'House of Israel' he said, 'can I not do to you as this potter does? ... Yes, as clay is in the potter's hand, so you are in mine, House of Israel' (Jeremiah 18:6). I love the idea that God can reshape us to be kinder, better people; perhaps Jeremiah should be named patron saint of rehab clinics, for we know that God can and does reshape alcoholics and drug addicts.

The other familiar story concerns the prophet Ezekiel who, in Chapter 37 of the book of his name, was carried by the hand of the Lord to visit a valley of bones. 'He made me walk up and down among them. There were vast quantities of these bones on the ground the whole length of the valley; and they were quite dried up' (Ezekiel 37:2). Yahweh instructed Ezekiel to prophesy over the bones and make them live. Ezekiel did as he is told and, to his utter amazement, there followed a noise, a sound of clattering, and the bones joined together. Not only did the bones reassemble themselves but they became re-clothed in sinews, muscle and flesh. Finally, God breathed life into them and they stood erect, an immense army of people.

The Valley of the Dry Bones reminded me of the mass graves found from time to time in Chile, Rwanda and other countries which have been ravaged by war. On a visit to the Atacama Desert a few years ago, our taxi passed an enormous iron cross standing by the desert road. A week later, as we returned to the airport, I asked the driver to stop at the cross and tell us what it marked. Reluctantly, he recounted the story that, in the early post-coup days of 1973, a team of army officers flew a helicopter up the coast north of Santiago. At each town, they stopped and detained anyone loyal to the defeated president, Doctor Salvador Allende, and, after a brief period of interrogation, executed those whom they judged to be a threat to the new regime. This purge came to be known as the 'Caravan de la Muerte', the 'Caravan of Death', and an account of those who died, in the words of their loved ones, was published in Barcelona in 2001. In total, seventy-five men were executed and twenty-six of them were disinterred in the desert between Calama and San Pedro de Atacama.

As I walked across the sand to look at the iron cross towering above me, I came upon a group of memorial stones and photographs of those who had died. Alongside the photographs was a motley of artificial flowers: the expression of a powerless grief, such as that we in the United Kingdom place on the roadside to mark the spots where our young motorcyclists die equally painful and pointless deaths.

Pray God that their bones will one day be covered again with flesh, so that they may be reunited with those who love them.

I cannot finish this lightning tour of the Old Testament without mention of two more of the prophets, Hosea and Micah. In the Book of Hosea, the prophet applies to the Israelites the imagery of an unfaithful wife. God's ways are not our ways: she does not reject sinners but pursues them to wherever, in their shame, they have gone to hide:

> 'that is why I am going to lure her and lead her out into the wilderness and speak to her heart.'
>
> Hosea 2:16

When that day comes, said the Lord,

'I will betroth you to myself forever,
Betroth you with integrity and justice, with tenderness and love;
I will betroth you to myself with faithfulness, and you will come
to know Yahweh.

Hosea 2:21–22

I find this imagery of brides and marriage mind-boggling: this is how
much our God loves us, and yet we are so cold, so distant. This to me is
what makes a nonsense of going to church on Sunday in one's best
clothes, as if visiting a maiden aunt. Our God is not like that: she is a
spouse, a partner to share our homes, our lives, our beds.

Like a young man marrying a virgin,
So will the one who built you wed you,
And as the bridegroom rejoices in his bride
So will your God rejoice in you.

Isaiah 62:5

Lastly, we come to Micah 6:6–8, the undeniable blueprint for the god-
fearing, which we so easily forget. The prophet asked what God
demanded of us, and heard more than he bargained for:

With what gifts shall I come into Yahweh's presence
And bow down before God's presence on high?
Shall I come with holocausts, with calves one year old?
Will he be pleased with rams by the thousand with libations of
oil in torrents?
Must I give my firstborn for what I have done wrong, the fruit
of my body, for my own sin?

What is good has been explained to you man; this is what
Yahweh asks of you:
Only this: to act justly, to love tenderly – and to walk humbly
with your God.

What an amazing fragment of wisdom that is: one of the nuggets of pure
gold to be found in this large complex book. Just what it means in
practice for each and every one of us lies at the heart of the Christian
quest – and the Jewish, Muslim, Hindu and Buddhist, and all the faiths
we know and, no doubt, more we do not.

Chapter 10

Finding God in the Psalms

Ah my dear angry Lord,
Since thou dost love, yet strike;
Cast down, yet help afford;
Sure I will do the like.

I will complain, yet praise;
I will bewail, approve:
And all my sour-sweet days
I will lament, and love.

'Bitter-Sweet' by George Herbert

It is 16 August, supposedly the middle of the summer, and the rain pours down in torrents while the wind howls in my ears. Today is surely a day for a moaning, complaining psalm, a petulant email to the Divine.

What are you up to, Lord?
What have you done with the sun?
Have you forgotten it's August?
Your people should be playing on the beach,
Not cowering under umbrellas.
The pools are empty: no swimmers today.
The cafes are closed:
Their owners go hungry.

Don't you care that the campers are drowning,
The rivers bursting their banks?
Blind, uncaring God
You are deaf to our cries,
Fast asleep and snoring
Like a wet dog on the sofa!

The psalms are cries from the heart: exclamations of joy, fury or distress. They are the songs of a people to whom God is so real, so close, that talking to him or her is completely natural. As I near my home after an evening out, I beg God to find me a parking space. 'You can do it, Lord!' I say, 'You know you can do it! *Please!*'

I don't pretend that this is a 'good' prayer, or that it is not supremely self-centred, but is the prayer of that moment, born of my need and childlike faith in an all-powerful God. Does God answer my prayer? I'm not really sure, but I have a sneaking suspicion, based on years of experience, that she does!

Prayers of petition come naturally to us, and so, of course, should the prayers of a grateful heart. When I spy a gap right in front of my house, my prayers of gratitude are ecstatic. 'Thank you Lord, thank you! You are *so* good to me!' As I weasel my way into a space that is barely long enough for my battered green Peugeot, I thank him again, for my luck, my parking success and for the joy in my heart.

The prayers of the psalmist are, of course, more serious and more poetic than mine, but they follow the same pattern: they are cries of anguish, of despair, of joy and of praise. I had the great good fortune to become steeped, 'pickled', in the psalms during my three years of monastic living. For those unfamiliar with monastic life, I should perhaps explain that men and women leading this form of life meet together five or six times a day to sing or recite the 'Divine Office': the collection of 150 psalms and various readings from the scripture. Over the years, these monks and nuns come to know many of the psalms by heart, so that fragments are released into the stream of the mind like twigs into a river. In this way, the psalms provide a sort of spiritual food for people to regurgitate, remember and reflect upon during the day.

One of my favourite snatches of poetry is Psalm 62 (the unwary reader should note that there are two systems for numbering the psalms: the number to be found in most Christian liturgies is taken from the Greek Septuagint, which is different from that found in the Hebrew text and the Authorised Version. Number 62 in the Gelineau translation is Number 63 in the Jerusalem Bible):

O God, you are my God, for you I long;
For you my soul is thirsting.
My body pines for you
Like a dry, weary land without water.
So I gaze on you in the sanctuary
To see your strength and your glory.
For your love is better than life,
My lips will seek your praise.

Psalm 63:1–3

This is without doubt a love song, full of wonderful imagery to convey the writer's deep intuitive knowledge that, without God, we shrivel and die. I know these words by heart and find myself reciting them sometimes when my mind is not crowded with work or trivia. It reminds me, as I write, of another favourite love poem, W. H. Auden's 'Funeral Blues' – also known by its famous first line, 'Stop all the clocks,' – recited so powerfully by John Hannah in the film *Four Weddings and a Funeral*.

As I consider these two poems, I wonder if there are those who would be outraged at my comparing a psalm with a lover's lament for his gay partner. Is the love of God 'good' and acceptable, albeit a little embarrassing when expressed so powerfully? And what about love between humans? Is the love of a mother for her child holy, the love of a husband for his wife wholesome, but the love between same-sex lovers disgusting?

Oh how very confused and bigoted we are. Do we not remember the words of St John in his first letter:

My dear people, Let us love one another since love comes from God
And everyone who loves is begotten by God and knows God.
Anyone who fails to love can never have known God because
God is love.

1 John 4:7

It occurs to me as I re-read this passage that people are not to be divided, as we are sometimes tempted, into Christians and non-believers, the saved and the damned (what an appalling concept), but rather into those who love and those who don't, or can't. John is so clear on this:

My dear people, since God has loved us so much
We too should love one another.

1 John 4:11

The psalms encompass a kaleidoscope of human emotions, from love and awe to fear and despair. A favourite of many of my friends, and indeed of mine, is Psalm 138, titled, in my Gelineau Psalter, 'The Hound of Heaven'. Here we have, once more, the theme of Divine call and the pursuit of the unwilling soul by an ever-faithful God.

> O Lord, you search me and you know me,
> you know my resting and my rising,
> you discern my purpose from afar.
> You mark when I walk or lie down.
> All my ways lie open to you.
> O where can I go from your spirit,
> or where can I flee from your face?
> If I climb the heavens you are there.
> If I lie in the grave, you are there.
> If I take the wings of the dawn
> and dwell at the sea's farthest end,
> Even there your hand would lead me,
> you right hand would hold me fast.
>
> Psalm 138:1–3, 7–10

I wonder how many people have experienced this sense of being pursued by the Divine? I myself felt hounded for over twenty years, from the time I first wondered if I had a 'vocation' to be a nun at the age of seventeen until the time I was asked to leave a convent in my mid-forties because I was so miserable. In some ways, it seems that I misunderstood what God wanted of me, but how else would I have been exposed to the scriptures and the Fathers of the Church? Whoever it was who said 'God writes straight with crooked lines' knew what she was talking about!

Today, at last, the sun is shining and I can feel its warmth on my back as I sit at my desk by the window. My Gelineau Psalter lies open at Psalm 103, a delightful eulogy to the Creator God. It begins in a pious sort of way:

> Bless the Lord, my soul
> Lord God how great you are …
>
> Psalm 103:1

but continues with a wonderfully poetic account of the creation of the Universe. This is not Darwin's story, nor yet a rigid creationist account, for it is full of wonder and joy, a contemplative countryman's observation. Here is another taster passage:

> From your dwelling you water the hills;
> earth drinks its fill of your gift.
> You make the grass grow for the cattle
> and the plants to serve man's needs,
> That he may bring forth bread from the earth
> And wine to cheer man's heart;
> The trees of the Lord drink their fill,
> the cedars he planted on Lebanon;
> There the birds build their nest:
> On the tree top the stork has her home.
> The goats find a home on the mountains
> And rabbits hide in the rocks.
>
> Psalm 103:13–18

As I write, it occurs to me that David Attenborough (a broadcaster well-known and much-loved in the United Kingdom for his stunning nature films) should read this psalm to us in that wonderful mellow voice with which he describes the antics of the creatures in his natural history programmes.:

> You made the moon to mark the months;
> The sun knows the time for its setting;
> When you spread the darkness it is night
> And all the beasts of the forest creep forth.
> The young lions roar for their prey,
> And ask for their food from God.
>
> Psalm 103:19–21

I wonder who wrote this psalm in particular? Are there lions in Israel? And forests: where are the forests? How little I know about this Promised Land and the men who wrote these words. There are echoes in this psalm of the last few chapters of the book of Job. The scenario here is the dialogue between Job, the good man brought low by illness and misfortune, and Yahweh, whom he has served faithfully all his life. Yahweh listens patiently as Job complains and then speaks out from the heart of the tempest:

Who is this obscuring my designs
With his empty-headed words?
Brace yourself like a fighter,
Now it is my turn to ask questions and yours to inform me.
Where were you when I laid the earth's foundations?
Tell me, since you are so well informed! …
Have you ever in your life given orders to the morning
Or sent the dawn to its post? …
Have you journeyed all the way to the sources of the sea,
Or walked where the Abyss is deepest?

Job 38:2–4, 12, 16

The psalmist, too, is awed by the sea:

> There is the sea, vast and wide,
> With its moving swarms past counting,
> Living things great and small.
> The ships are moving there
> And the monsters you made to play with.
>
> Psalm 103:25–26

I love the image of God playing with his monsters: the whale, the shark
and the porpoise, those amazing denizens of the deep. In my mind's eye I
am reminded of magical films of a lithe, silver-clad young woman 'free
diver', who dives to incredible depths without apparatus or oxygen, and
swims with dolphins and even with a mother whale and her calf.

The last few stanzas of this psalm speak of all creatures' utter dependence upon God; a lesson learned, no doubt, as we have learned it, from
drought, earthquake and tsunami:

> All of these look to you
> To give them their food in due season.
> You give it, they gather it up:
> You open your hand, they have their fill.
> You hide your face, they are dismayed;
> You take back your spirit, they die,
> Returning to the dust from which they came.
> You send forth your spirit, they are created;
> And you renew the face of the earth.
>
> Psalm 103:27–30

How easy it is to forget our dependence on the unseen God – and how convenient. Perhaps being a doctor makes me more aware of our vulnerability, for I have watched so many men and women take their last breath; *ruah* (Hebrew for 'breath, spirit') – it is pure gift. The Lord gives and takes away: that we know, but oh, how hard it is to praise her when she withdraws her spirit.

Psalm 90 puts all thought of the God who takes away on the back burner, and rejoices in a childlike trust in the Divine. This psalm is sung at Compline, the night prayer of the Church wherever monks and nuns sink their roots. The first verse is familiar to most churchgoers:

He who dwells in the shelter of the Most High
And abides in the shade of the Almighty
Says to the Lord 'My refuge, my stronghold, my God in whom I trust.'

Compline is perhaps my favourite service of the Divine Office. During my eighteen months at Ampleforth, I would listen for the tolling of the bell and then make my way to the church. A peace and stillness would descend upon the assembled monks and lay people as they left behind the cares of the day and prepared for the Grand Silence, which would follow the service. No matter that the teaching monks would return wearily to their piles of exercise books, or to rowdy boarders unwilling to go to bed. At least they could silence the mind's turmoil for half an hour, if not for the whole evening.

As I write now, I am ambivalent about the words of this psalm: I believe it, and yet I know it to be wishful thinking. We all long for peace in the evening, for sleep when we are tired, but each day, for some, that peace will be shattered by gunfire, smoke or earthquake. Political prisoners are snatched at night; babies in their cots stop breathing for no good reason; drunken youths stab each other on the streets of our cities. Perhaps, then, Psalm 90 is a plea to God to spare us from the terrors of the night, made by a people who are all too aware of their vulnerability.

'Save us Lord,' we sing in the Antiphon, 'while we are awake: protect us while we are asleep: that we may watch with Christ and rest peacefully.'

It's curious that we love these psalms of trust and confidence so much despite their ostrich, head-in-the-sand quality. Psalm 22 (known more popularly as Psalm 23) is an all-time favourite:

The lord is my shepherd;
There is nothing I shall want ...
If I should walk in the valley of darkness no evil would I fear.

I find this lovely, yet theologically and practically untrue; try singing it to the flood victims, to the man whose child was washed away, or to the victims of the latest stabbing or arson attack. And yet, as I reflect upon my own experience of the dark valley of torture and solitary confinement, I have to acknowledge that I never felt that God had abandoned me; just that we were suffering together. Similarly, Irina Ratushinskaya was shown her 'upheaval of rainbow ice' in a Siberian prison cell, and Dietrich Bonhoeffer retained his faith in God whilst awaiting execution by the Nazis.

> I believe that God will give us all the strength that we need to cope with what he sends, but he doesn't give it in advance lest we take it for granted.
>
> Dietrich Bonhoeffer

More powerful and more challenging by far than the twenty-third psalm is Psalm 101, a terrifying lament of the man imprisoned or dying from cancer.

> O Lord listen to my prayer
> And let my cry for help reach you.
> Do not hide your face from me
> In the day of my distress.
>
> For my days are vanishing like smoke,
> My bones burn away like a fire.
> My heart is withered like the grass.
> I forget to eat my bread.
> I have become like a pelican in the wilderness,
> Like an owl in desolate places.
> I lie awake and I moan
> Like some lonely bird on a roof.
>
> Psalm 101:1–7

Half way through, the psalm changes into a song of praise and trust in God, but the last two stanzas return to the psalmist's initial anguish:

He has broken my strength in mid-course;
He has shortened the days of my life.
I say to God: do not take me away
Before my days are complete,
You, whose days last from age to age.

Psalm 101:23–24

I love the courage of the psalmist who challenges Yahweh with the injustice of his plight, comparing it with God's eternal life: 'You neither change nor have an end,' he declares, acknowledging the gulf between himself and his creator.

I like this psalm because it is real, because the psalmist utters his bitter truth without apology. No sugar-coated piety here, just a desperate cry for help. I have been like the pelican in the wilderness and I have spent my life caring for those whose strength is broken in mid-course, whose days have been shortened for no apparent reason. Life is uncertain. Life is hard. Trusting God is one thing, kidding oneself that one will walk through the dark valley unscathed is something else.

There are 150 psalms and I have quoted but a few to tempt you to reach for a Psalter. They are best sung: it's almost (but not quite) a reason to enter monastic life. The next best thing is to read them to yourself until they are familiar, and then, of course, you may have the courage, like my friend Carla Piette, to write one:

Waters of mountains; waters of God
Cleanse us, renew us, so shabbily shod.
Rivers of Chile, streams of burnt snow
Melt us, tow us, beyond friend or foe.
Currents so fast, pools deep and clear
Tune us, quiet our hearts still to hear.
Lord of the river, God of the stream
Teach us your song, our dryness redeem.

Carla wrote this in Chile in 1976. In 1980 she was drowned in a river in El Salvador (as I described in Chapter 7). I find her 'psalm' quite spooky. Holy God, we do not understand your ways.

Chapter 11

Finding God in the Gospels

I find it strangely difficult to move on from the Old Testament and the Psalms to the Gospels, possibly because it's the poetry in the previous writings which I love so much. The Gospels are the stories of Jesus of Nazareth, a preacher who lived two millennia ago and whom many people understand to be the Son of God. As I wrote this rather diffident statement, my mind was suddenly assailed by fragments of verse: 'And is it true? And is it true … That God was man in Palestine, And lives today in Bread and Wine.'

At first I thought it must be by Francis Thompson or Hilaire Belloc, but I searched vainly in their anthologies. Next I tried the Dictionary of Quotations, but my search was again in vain. Then it suddenly came to me: it was John Betjeman, and I knew I'd find it in his poem, 'Christmas'.

So: is it true? *Was* God man in Palestine? Was Jesus of Nazareth the Son of God in a uniquely special, mysterious way, or was he another holy man, a preacher and a prophet? Ten years ago, I'd have said that of course Jesus was God made man. Now, to be truthful, I don't know. My personal faith draws me to worship the mysterious unseen God, the creator of the Universe – a faith which I believe I share with many members of the other 'Great Religions'. I have no deep personal devotion to Jesus as Lord, as so many Christians have, but I do have devotion to the teachings of Jesus, the four Gospels. I mean by this that I believe that they are wise and true and inspired by God, and, most importantly, that, studied in conjunction with the Old Testament, they form a unique blueprint for right living.

I have to admit, at this juncture, that such familiarity as I may have with the scriptures is entirely dependent upon the Catholic Church and my sixty-odd years of churchgoing. The liturgies of the Sunday Mass include two scripture readings and in religious community life, of course, the exposure is much greater, as each 'office' is made up of psalms and scripture. In monastic communities, there is another mode of exposure to the scriptures in the practice known as Lectio Divina. This is a private reading of scripture, in which a short passage is read and re-read slowly and thoughtfully until all the sweetness and meaning has been sucked out: rather like eating a grape. It is a very different process to sitting and listening to a passage being read in church, either well or badly. As in the singing of the psalms, this slow meditative reading of the scriptures on a regular basis produces a deep familiarity with the Word of God and, hopefully, an understanding of its messages.

Enough of introductions; let us begin at the beginning: the birth of the child Jesus in Bethlehem. I'm sure I don't need to retell this story, which is somehow embedded in our culture. It is always useful, however, to approach the very familiar from a new direction, and to do this I sometimes like to consider T. S. Eliot's poem, 'The Journey of the Magi'. The Magi were Three Wise Men who came to seek out the child whom their books had foretold would be born in Bethlehem. They would have been familiar with two particular passages from Isaiah:

> The Lord himself, therefore,
> Will give you a sign.
> It is this: the maiden is with child
> And will soon give birth to a son
> Whom she will call Immanuel.
>
> Isaiah 7:14

> A shoot springs from the stock of Jesse,
> A scion thrusts from his roots:
> On him the spirit of Yahweh rests,
> A spirit of wisdom and insight,
> A spirit of counsel and power,
> A spirit of knowledge and the fear of Yahweh.
>
> Isaiah 11:1–2

Eliot, in his poem, captures the world of the Magi in a way that no crib set ever can: I value his poem because it is so brilliantly empathic without being in the least bit sentimental. In it we have no frankincense and myrrh, but three puzzled men, not sure exactly what they had witnessed – 'were we led all that way for Birth or Death?' – yet convinced that it was something hugely important, something life-changing. Never again would they be at home 'in the old dispensation', for their eyes had been cruelly opened to the reality of their world 'with an alien people clutching their gods.'

There is little told of Jesus' childhood in the Gospels, except the story of his 'presentation' in the temple, and the account of how he went missing for several hours and was found eventually talking to the elders. More significant for me is the account of his 'debut' as a preacher, an occasion which I have referred to in an earlier chapter. The story is told in Luke 4:14:

> Jesus, with the power of the Spirit in him, returned to Galilee;
> and his reputation spread throughout the countryside. He
> taught in their synagogues and everyone praised him.

He travelled to Nazareth, where he had been brought up, and went to worship in the synagogue. It was there that they handed him the scroll of the prophet Isaiah and he chose to read the prophet's account of his call:

> 'The spirit of the Lord has been given to me,
> For he has anointed me.
> He has sent me to bring the good news to the poor,
> (To heal the broken hearted,)
> To proclaim liberty to captives
> And to the blind new sight,
> To set the downtrodden free,
> To proclaim the Lord's year of favour.'
> Luke 4:18–19 (quoting Isaiah 61:1, 8)

He handed back the scroll to the assistant and began to preach. 'This text,' he said, 'is being fulfilled today even as you listen'.

So: what can we learn about Jesus from this account of St Luke? Firstly, we can assume that Jesus was well versed in the Hebrew scriptures, and that he was an eloquent preacher. Next, and more controversially, we hear him apply this passage of Isaiah to himself.

You will note, if you read the paragraphs that follow the one I have quoted, that although Jesus was initially praised for his eloquence, that praise turned quickly to anger when he likened himself to the prophet Elijah. 'Everyone in the synagogue was enraged', and they 'hustled him out of town' (Luke 4:28–29). Jesus, however, gave them the slip – after all, this was just the beginning of his ministry.

What strikes me about this episode, as I have written earlier, is the content of the passage from Isaiah which Jesus chose. It is pure human rights teaching; the poor are to be given what belongs rightfully to them and the captives set free. Oxfam and Amnesty could not have put it better. Jesus, through his reading of Isaiah, proclaims 'the Lord's year of favour'.

In this, he is referring to the teaching to be found in the book of Leviticus, that every fiftieth year shall be called a Year of Jubilee: 'You will declare this fiftieth year sacred and proclaim the liberation of all the inhabitants of the land' (Leviticus 25:8).

I remember now the campaign organised by some of the Christian Non-governmental Organisations to proclaim the year 2000 a Jubilee year. The idea was that the richer nations of the world should cancel the debts of the poorer ones, so that the latter might be given the chance of liberating their own downtrodden masses.

In the weeks and months that followed, Jesus performed a number of 'miracles': he drove a demon out of a man in the temple and cured a lady of a high fever. His cures impressed people, and reports of him went through all the surrounding countryside.

At the end of Luke Chapter 4, we are told that Jesus left the house at dawn and made his way to a lonely place, presumably to pray. We can observe this pattern throughout the Gospels – Jesus deliberately sought solitude after periods of active ministry, a way of life which the Jesuits (followers of Jesus) would describe as a life of action underpinned, sustained, by periods of contemplation.

When the crowds he had impressed by his cures sought him out and wanted to prevent him from leaving, he answered that he must move on, because he had been sent to proclaim the 'Good News' of the Kingdom to other towns.

The Bible has its own 'jargon' which is sometimes hard to understand. I struggled particularly hard to understand Jesus' notion of the 'Kingdom of God and the Good News'. I don't recall if I ended up with a clear definition, but my understanding now is that the 'Kingdom' is God present in the here and now of our lives. As the prophesy puts it:

> Immanuel, God with us.
> The Lord himself, therefore, will give you a sign.
> It is this: the maiden is with child
> And will soon give birth to a son whom she will call Immanuel.
> Isaiah 7:14

We glimpse it too in the prophecy of the shoot that sprang from the stock of Jesse, the man on whom the spirit of the Lord rested. There follows a lyrical description of how he will rule and the peace of his Kingdom:

> He does not judge by appearance, he gives no verdict on hearsay, but judges the wretched with integrity and with equity gives a verdict for the poor of the land.
> Isaiah 11:3–4

More familiar to most of us is Isaiah's description of paradise, or the Messianic Kingdom:

> The wolf lives with the lamb,
> The panther lies down with the kid,
> Calf and lion cub feed together
> With a little boy to lead them.
> Isaiah 11:6

Is this what Jesus means by the Kingdom? Or was he planting seeds of hope and justice, teaching a way of life in which tiny islands of the Kingdom will coalesce to make a better world?

Jesus knew that he could not carry out his mission single-handed, and he proceeded to select helpers from the people around him. Note that he did not put up an advertisement in the synagogue, nor did he call for volunteers from the congregation. No. He followed God's time-honoured method and called the unsuitable by name, telling them to put their lives on hold, pack up their businesses and follow him. Here we have the call of Simon and the sons of Zebedee, James and John, the fishermen whose boat Jesus commandeered to teach the crowds. After he had finished preaching, Jesus told the men to put their boats out into deeper water. The men argued; they had fished all night and caught nothing. They *knew* that there were no fish about; but, to please Jesus, they put out their nets. I expect you know the story: they caught so many fish that the nets tore and the boats began to sink. Simon was overwhelmed by the experience and fell on his knees, saying: 'Leave me Lord; I am a sinful man.' Poor Simon; little did he know that God makes a habit of calling sinners to do his work, of reworking misshapen pots to carry precious wine.

Jesus said to Simon:

> 'Do not be afraid: from now on it is men you will catch'. Then, bringing their boats back to land, they left everything and followed him.
>
> Luke 5:1–11

There's another 'call' story later on in Chapter 5 of Luke, when Jesus noticed a tax collector sitting by the customs house and said to him: 'Follow me!' In our modern world, where the tax collectors go incognito lest we vent our wrath upon them, we could imagine Jesus calling a traffic warden in the act of putting a parking ticket on some poor unsuspecting man's car.

We are told that Levi, the tax collector, threw a party for Jesus and, not unreasonably, invited a group of workmates. The Scribes and the Pharisees (perhaps the equivalent of the parish council?) objected, and asked the disciples what Jesus thought he was doing eating with tax collectors and sinners. Jesus' jaw-dropping reply is worthy of our study:

> 'I have not come to call the virtuous, but sinners to repentance.'
>
> Luke 5:32

If Jesus were alive today, I wonder, would he work with young offenders or alcoholics, or perhaps with child molesters? My guess is that he'd see these people not so much as sinners but as wounded souls, in need of a healer's skills. Here, in the solitude of my flat, I hear in my mind the exasperations of those who complain: 'Social workers! Social workers!

They always excuse people by saying their mothers didn't love them or their fathers beat the living daylights out of them. Why can't criminals take responsibility for their crimes instead of blaming it all on their parents?' Not only does Jesus fraternise with tax collectors and prostitutes, but he has the audacity to tell his listeners to love their enemies!

> 'Love your enemies, do good to those who hate you, bless those who curse you, pray for those who treat you badly. To the man who slaps you on one cheek, present the other cheek too; to the man who takes your cloak from you, do not refuse your tunic.'
>
> Luke 6:27–29

I must admit that I find this instruction to love my enemies and turn the other cheek hard to swallow. No wonder Jesus antagonised the authorities, who no doubt enjoyed punishing their enemies.

Much easier to understand and try to practice is his instruction on compassion and judgement:

> 'Be compassionate as your Father is compassionate. Do not judge, and you will not be judged yourselves; do not condemn and you will not be condemned yourselves; grant pardon and you will be pardoned. Give and there will be gifts for you; a full measure, pressed down, shaken together, and running over, will be poured into your lap; because the amount you measure out is the amount you will be given back.'
>
> Luke 6:36–38

I really love this last passage of timeless wisdom and see it as being at the heart of the Christian message. As a certified shopaholic, being generous with unwanted (and wanted) plunder is the only way to survive, and sharing of things with my friends and neighbours has become second nature. I gave an unneeded armchair to Michael and Marcia (who are natural minimalists) when they moved in next door. Now Marcia brings me fresh fruit and vegetables grown by her ninety-year-old vicar Dad, who give *her* more than she needs when she goes to visit. At the moment, I have fresh lettuce literally pressed down and running over in my fridge, and must remember to take the remains of the duck to Michael, who, though a Zen monk, is still a carnivore. All this must surely be spiritual progress from the day of my twelfth birthday, when I hid my birthday cake in the cupboard in case the visitors (no doubt bearing gifts) should eat it all up!

If you turn the pages of Luke or the other Gospels as I am doing now, you will see that Jesus seemed to divide his time between teaching and working miracles of a healing nature. Sometimes it seemed he even raised the dead, like the daughter of Jairus in Luke 8:40–56, or his friend Lazarus, who was literally decomposing in John 11:1–43. I'm not really sure what we modern sceptics are supposed to make of such supernatural feats but, perhaps, because they are so familiar, I find them less exciting than Jesus' teaching.

Some time along his three-year journey to Calvary, Jesus prophesied his own death and resurrection, telling his disciples that he, the Son of Man, was destined to suffer grievously, to be rejected by the elders and the chief priests and scribes and put to death, and raised up on the third day.

What, I wonder, is going on here: did Jesus really prophesy his own death *and* his resurrection, or has this bit been inserted by the evangelist or a later writer? I can understand that Jesus might foresee that the religious authorities would only tolerate him for so long, but to think of him calmly prophesying his own resurrection (John 2:19–22 and Luke 9:22) sends shivers up my spine. In the passage from John, the prophecy follows the scene where Jesus made a whip out of some cord and drove the merchants and the money-lenders, along with their chickens and pigeons, out of the Temple. He scattered the money-changers' coins, knocked their tables over and commanded the pigeon sellers to stop turning his Father's house into a market.

When the Jews challenged him and asked him for a sign to justify what he had done, Jesus answered: 'Destroy this sanctuary and in three days I will raise it up.' Jesus, of course, was speaking not of the Temple but of his own body. This theme of Jesus as the sanctuary is picked up in the vision of the messianic Jerusalem in the book of Revelation:

> I saw that there was no temple in the city since the Lord God Almighty and the Lamb were themselves the temple and the city did not need the sun or moon for light, since it was lit by the radiant glory of God and the Lamb was a lighted torch for it.
>
> Revelation 21:22–23

I don't pretend to understand the symbols used in the book of Revelation but I cannot but be awed at this image of the Divine, a light which eclipses the sun, moon and stars: the radiant glory of God.

Whether Jesus really prophesied his resurrection after three days we shall never know: but what we can know is that these men who wrote about their Lord and master were convinced that he was God's anointed Son and that he rose from the dead.

In almost the same breath as he talked of his own death, Jesus warned his disciples that they must prepare themselves, because anyone who followed him would be bound to suffer:

> To all he said 'If anyone wants to be a follower of mine, let him renounce himself and take up his cross every day and follow me. For anyone who wants to save his life will lose it, but anyone who loses his life for my sake will save it.'
>
> Luke 9:23–24

It makes me laugh weakly to think of that passage in relation to this popular prayer:

> Gentle Jesus, meek and mild,
> Look on me, a little child.

There was nothing meek or mild about the man Jesus and we do neither him nor ourselves a favour by thinking of him as a mild-mannered, asexual being. Jesus of Nazareth, Son of God or not, was certainly fully human.

As I bring this chapter to a close, I have deliberately chosen not to write about Jesus' Passion and his death on the cross. This is not because it is not important but because I find it too painful. As a Roman Catholic for more than seventy years, I have participated in more Good Friday liturgies than I can remember and I have walked the 'Stations of the Cross' many times. For many years this was, for me, a spiritual exercise which made me thoughtful, sad and perhaps a little guilty for my sins. Then, one Good Friday in Chile, I found my thoughts of Jesus' suffering violently intruded upon by thoughts of a man I knew who had just been arrested by the secret police. Entering, mentally, into what was probably happening to him made me feel so ill that I nearly threw up. It suddenly seemed irrelevant to try to imagine what was happening to Jesus two thousand years ago when someone I knew was probably being tortured at that very minute.

A few months later, I myself was arrested by the secret police for daring to give medical attention to a wounded revolutionary. Like Jesus, like all victims of torture throughout the ages, I was stripped naked, hurt and humiliated by men who clearly got some pleasure out of what they were doing. Since that time, I have deliberately avoided all portrayals of violence, whether they be in church or on the screen, because they revive the mental and bodily memories of what happened when I was weak and vulnerable. Torture is an unspeakable, gross violation of human rights and we must all work as best we can to rid it from the face of our God-given earth.

If I can't write about the Crucifixion I will end with the Last Supper, and I deliberately choose the Johannine version because I find it more instructive; it is an amazing legacy of the man Jesus.

It is a curious fact that, although the three Synoptic Gospels (Matthew, Mark and Luke) each devote a brief paragraph to the institution of the Eucharist, John does not mention it at all. Instead he describes a moving ceremony in which Jesus washes his disciples' feet, an action through which he models how they are to act when he has gone:

> 'Do you understand', he said, 'what I have done to you? You call
> me Master and Lord, and rightly; so I am. If I then, the
> Lord and Master, have washed your feet, you should wash each
> other's feet – I have given you an example so that you may copy
> what I have done to you.'
>
> John 13:2–20

I mentioned briefly, in Chapter Two, the hymn 'Will You Let Me Be Your Servant', written by Richard Gillard. Well, I reckon Jesus would have loved this hymn as much as I do, for surely it is his theme tune. It seems to me to be a blueprint for pastoral ministry, whether for priests, nuns or doctors; and it is, of course, born of a deep empathy, the key to all caring.

The authors of the Synoptic Gospels moved swiftly on from the Last Supper to Gethsemane, and all the horror that was to follow. John, however, took four chapters to tell the story of the Last Supper discourse, his farewell message to his disciples. I am no scripture scholar, so I cannot account for this difference; I merely draw your attention to four of the richest chapters in the Gospels.

'My little children,' Jesus began, 'I shall not be with you much longer.' You can imagine the disciples' cries of distress, for they were enjoying a Passover meal, not preparing for the cold-blooded murder of their leader. I can imagine him hushing their protests so that he could give them the most important advice of their lives:

'I give you a new commandment:
Love one another: just as I have loved you,
You also must love one another.
By this love you have for one another,
Everyone will know that you are my disciples.'

John 13:34–35

Perhaps you should lay this book down now for a while, because nothing else I say can add to this message.

In the passages of John which follow – Chapters 14 to 17 – Jesus spoke in a way that he had not spoken before. In particular, he spoke of his relationship with God, whom he calls the Father. In response to Thomas' question, 'How can we know the way?' (to follow him), Jesus made one of his most beautiful and mysterious statements:

'I am the Way, the Truth and the Life.
No one can come to the Father except through me.
If you know me, you know my Father too.
From this moment you know him and have seen him.'

John 14:6–7

The disciples were mystified. They don't know about the Trinity and what Jesus was saying was hard to understand. Philip said, reasonably enough: 'Lord, let us see the Father and then we shall be satisfied.' Jesus, perhaps, sighed, and explained:

'To have seen me is to have seen the Father, so how can you say "Let us see the Father?" Do you not believe that I am in the Father and the Father is in me?'

John 14:9–10

Jesus went on to talk about the Advocate, or Holy Spirit, and the disciples were even more perplexed.

The chapters that follow are not easy to understand, in that they are about Jesus' relationship with his Father. Embedded in them, however, are a number of familiar lines; many of them words of comfort:

'I will not leave you orphans; I will come back to you.'

John 14:18

'Peace I bequeath to you, my own peace I give you, a peace that the world cannot give, this is my gift to you. Do not let your hearts be troubled or afraid.'

John 14:27

In Chapter 15 he gave the disciples the image of the vine:

'I am the true vine, and my Father is the vinedresser …
Make your home in me, as I make mine in you.
As a branch cannot bear fruit all by itself,
But must remain part of the Vine,
Neither can you unless you remain in me.
I am the Vine, you are the branches.
Whoever remains in me, with me in him, bears fruit in plenty;
For cut off from me you can do nothing.'

John 15:1, 4–5

If theologians, learned and wise, have difficulty deciphering the meaning of these and the other verses of Jesus' Last Supper discourse, I wonder what the disciples made of it all. They were fishermen and tax collectors, not university graduates, and they were struggling with the news that Jesus was about to leave them. There were no tape recorders; John wrote down what he remembered many years later. Nevertheless, these are amazing texts which merit study at a closer and deeper level.

After the supper, Jesus went to pray in the Garden of Gethsemane – and you know the rest. He was arrested, beaten, tried and executed. The disciples were terrified and ran away; only his mother, Mary, and John kept vigil with him as he died on the cross.

On the third day after his death, Jesus' body vanished from the tomb. He was seen, we are told, by Mary of Magdala, and, later, by the disciples who were convinced that Jesus had died and risen again.

Chapter 12

Finding God in Poetry

When I speak about 'finding' God in poetry, I mean that certain poems fill me with a sense of the Divine: a sense of awe and of love.

As in painting or sculpture, a man or woman's taste in poetry is always personal. I have to admit that most of Shakespeare leaves me cold. But other verse, and occasionally prose, produces in me a sense akin to ecstasy. Alas, I must limit myself in this chapter to around ten or so 'Desert Island' favourites and leave the others for an anthology to be compiled possibly one day in the future.

Before I begin my selection, I must say a word about the language that different people use to speak about God. Like poetry, this language is intensely personal and words which thrill the heart of one person will make another feel uneasy, if not positively 'sick'. I believe that it is really important that we understand these differences, because if we don't, we are likely to write off our neighbour's God as an idol.

Let me give you an example. My favourite prayer, which I suspect comes from the Orthodox liturgy, is:

> Holy God,
> Holy and strong,
> Holy and deathless
> Have mercy on us.

A similar prayer, also used as a type of mantra, is the Russian Orthodox Jesus Prayer:

> Lord Jesus Christ,
> Son of the living God,
> Have mercy on me a sinner.

I think I prefer the former prayer, because it is powerfully *theocentric*, – focused upon the powerful, unseen, transcendent God, while the second one is *Christocentric*, focused on the redemptive powers of Christ. It's not that I am no longer a Christian, or that I do not believe in the Incarnation or Resurrection, because I am and I do. Nevertheless, my feelings of devotion are aroused more by that which I cannot see or imagine, than that which I can.

The power of poetry in the spiritual context lies in its use of images that arouse our sense of the Divine in an oblique, rather than a direct, way. Let us take as an example the Jesuit poet Gerard Manley Hopkins' poem, 'The Windhover', and compare it with the simple prayer:

> Gentle Jesus, meek and mild,
> Look on me, a little child.

Listen to Hopkins:

> I caught this morning morning's minion, king-
> dom of daylight's dauphin, dapple-dawn-drawn Falcon, in his riding
> Of the rolling level underneath him steady air, and striding
> High there, how he rung upon the rein of a wimpling wing
> In his ecstasy!

Hopkins was at St Beuno's Theological College when he wrote this poem in May 1877, and I can imagine him standing, exhilarated and awed, as he watched the falcon in flight and likened its power, freedom and beauty to that of the risen Christ.

The first poem/prayer, as I mentioned in the previous chapter, is far too sentimental for my taste. My understanding of Jesus of Nazareth is that he was a feisty, valiant man and no more 'meek and mild' than I am.

I lay down my Hopkins anthology for Karen Armstrong's anthology, 'Tongues of Fire', and, curiously, it falls open at another Hopkins poem, which just happens to be my favourite. I am speaking here of 'The Wreck of the Deutschland', inspired by a newspaper report of the wreck of a ship bearing a group of German nuns to their mission:

Thou mastering me,
God! giver of breath and bread,
World's strand, sway of the sea,
Lord of living and dead;
Thou hast bound bones and veins in me, fastened me flesh,
And after it almost unmade, what with dread
Thy doing: and dost thou touch me afresh?
Over again I feel thy finger and find thee.

There are few words adequate to write of a battle with God, and even fewer to describe facing a violent death at sea. There is no place either for a mild and gentle Jesus here, only fear and a prayer for courage:

This is a long poem and hard to fathom, so I quote only fragments.

The frown of his face
Before me, the hurtle of hell
Behind, where, where was a, where was a place?

Verse five is much gentler and one which I particularly love:

I kiss my hand
To the stars, lovely-asunder
Starlight, wafting him out of it; and
Glow, glory in thunder;
Kiss my hand to the dappled-with-damson west:
Since, tho' he is under the world's splendour and wonder,
His mystery must be instressed, stressed;
For I greet him the days that I meet him, and bless when I understand.

How blind are those who label the love of God in nature, pantheism; as blind as those who think we can summon up God like the Good Fairy, or a genie in a bottle. As Hopkins says so simply:

I greet him the days I meet him
And bless when I understand.

In the back of my Gelineau Psalter, last in use thirty years and more ago when I was a guest at Ampleforth Abbey, I have stuck two poems. One is by George Scott Moncrieff, and echoes my meeting God in nature theme:

Lord I you love in antrin things,
Rooks turning, wheeling, cawing in the sky.
Feathers of meadow grasses and soft feeling
Of gentle rain upon my face.
The howl and gauntlet hurling of a wind
Rising from nowhere, blowing whither no-one knows
Great waves that dash
Themselves to pieces on rocks ravaged by time
And many million storms.
Lord, I you love in fellowship
In bitter tears and laughter after all
Yet I do know Lord I shall love you best
When the ultimate time-struggles cease
And I with all the weight of my iniquity
Dropped off at last may look on you in peace.

The last couple of lines work for me less well, for I come from a school of
Christian belief which no longer dwells upon our sinfulness and inad-
equacy in the face of the Divine.

In contrast to this is a poem by Ralph Wright OSB, one of the monks of
Ampleforth Abbey, now living in the USA. It is entitled 'Messiah':

Messiah
anoint the wounds
of my spirit
with the balm
of forgiveness

pour the oil
of your calm
on the waters
of my heart

take the squeal
of frustration
from the wheels
of my passion
that the power
of your tenderness
may smooth
the way I love

that the tedium
of giving
in the risk
of surrender
and the reaching
out naked
to a world
that must wound

may be kindled
fresh daily
to a blaze
of compassion
that the grain
may fall gladly
to burst in the ground
– and the harvest abound.

Ralph's is a poem of our time, deeply psychologically aware of the cost, in stress and irritation, of the constant giving involved in the following of the Christian vocation. I have no patience with sentimental talk about Jesus, Christ and God the Father. Jesus was God's son, but he was truly human and lived his life as a member of the society of men and women of his time. All the simpering paintings of the 'pale Galilean', exposing his broken heart or knocking at the door of mine, do nothing for me. I have no need to see the long dead Jesus; indeed, human images get in the way of my knowing the man through his words and actions.

I am always irritated by those who use the terms Jesus and Christ interchangeably. My understanding of the Christian mystery is that the man Jesus died, as must we all, but rose again as the Christ, deathless, and invincible.

My theologian friends, if they ever read this, will smile at my floundering about, yet again, in mystery of the Trinity. Of course I don't understand it, that's what mystery is about. All I can do is return once more to Hopkins, and the second stanza of his poem 'God's Grandeur':

And for all this, nature is never spent;
There lives the dearest freshness deep down things;
And though the last lights off the black West went
Oh, morning, at the brown brink eastward, springs—
Because the Holy Ghost over the bent
World broods with warm breast and with ah! bright wings.

Enough of God in nature. Let us turn to R. S. Thomas, and an extract from his poem 'The Absence':

> It is a room I enter
> from which someone has just
> gone, the vestibule for the arrival
> of one who has not yet come.

What is it about those of us who are more excited by *absence* than *presence*? Why do I find God more easily in empty churches than full ones? Ann Lewin, I think, is a kindred spirit. Her poem, 'Disclosure':

> Prayer is like watching for the Kingfisher.
> All you can do is
> Be where he is likely to appear, and
> Wait.
> Often, nothing much happens;
> There is space, silence and
> Expectancy.
> No visible sign, only the
> Knowledge that he's been there,
> And may come again.
> Seeing or not seeing cease to matter,
> You have been prepared.
> But sometimes, when you've almost
> Stopped expecting it,
> A flash of brightness
> Gives encouragement.

Free association sends me instantly back to my dog-eared copy of Annie Dillard's *Pilgrim at Tinker Creek*:

> The secret of seeing is, then, the pearl of great price. If I thought he could teach me to find it and keep it forever I would stagger barefoot across a hundred deserts after any lunatic at all.

Later in the book, she writes of Moses:

> Moses said to God 'I beseech thee, shew me thy glory'. And God said 'Thou canst not see my face: for there shall no man see me, and live'.

You will remember the story, from Exodus 33:18–24. God put Moses in a cleft of the rock and shielded him with his hand while his 'glory' passed by, so that Moses glimpsed his 'back parts'.

'Just a glimpse, Moses,' says Dillard,

> a cleft in the rock here, a mountain top there, and the rest is denial and longing. You have to stalk everything. Everything scatters and gathers; everything comes and goes like fish under a bridge. You have to stalk the spirit too.

I remember back some years ago to conversations I had with my mentors at Ampleforth Abbey, and later with Gordon Mursell, then chaplain at the School of Theology in Salisbury, now a bishop in the Midlands. They spoke of two distinct ways of understanding the Divine mysteries: the *cataphatic* and the *apophatic*. Alas, I do not have the knowledge to define these words accurately, nor can I find them in my dictionary. I have only my memory of what was explained to me many years ago. Cataphatic theology concerns all we think we can say of God: that he is good and holy, loving and jealous, all-powerful, all knowing, omnipotent, omniscient and omnipresent. The apophatic way is in direct contrast. It holds God to be unknowable, unreachable and invisible; infinitely mysterious.

I have long been excited by the notion of the apophatic way, the way of unknowing. It is what makes most sense to me, because as the years go by I use fewer and fewer words when I pray. The darkness, too, is more conducive, for me, to prayer than the light.

Many years ago, when on retreat at Hopkins' old college, St Beuno, in North Wales, I would delight to pray face down on the floor in a darkened chapel. This seemed to me the most appropriate way to present myself before the Throne. Those days are now long gone, and now I sit by the sea, neither thinking nor speaking, but just being there: drinking my coffee, stroking my dogs and focussing on the Mystery.

Leafing through my Commonplace Book, I am reminded of a poem which spoke deeply to me in Chile. I'm sure I have quoted it in some other book, now long out of print, so I dare to present it here again. It was written by a missionary sister called Carol Bialock, and I don't think it has ever been published. I was so fascinated by it when she gave it to me that I took it into work at the hospital and re-read it from time to time. When I was arrested, it was in the top pocket of my white coat in my locker, from which place of safe-keeping, Derek Fernyhough, the British Consul, kindly rescued it for me. Carol, too, found the ocean a powerful image for speaking of the Divine:

I built my house by the sea.
Not on the sands, mind you, not on the shifting sand.
And I built it of rock.
A strong house
by a strong sea.
And we got well acquainted, the sea and I.
Good neighbours.
Not that we spoke much.
We met in silences,
respectful, keeping our distance
but looking our thoughts across the fence of sand.
Always the fence of sand our barrier,
always the sand between.
Then one day
(and I still don't know how it happened)
the sea came.
Without warning.
Without welcome even.
Not sudden and swift, but a shifting across the sand like wine
Less like the flow of water than the flow of blood.
Slow, but flowing like an open wound.
And I thought of flight, and I thought of drowning, and I thought of death.
But while I thought the sea crept higher till it reached my door.
And I knew that there was neither flight nor death nor drowning.
That when the sea comes calling you stop being good neighbours,
Well acquainted, friendly from distance neighbours,
and you give your house for a coral castle
And you learn to breathe under water.

Like most poems, this can be interpreted in different ways. The sea is clearly God; or is it? Perhaps it's the pain of the world which overwhelms those who work with the dispossessed. It's that image again of churchgoing in one's best clothes on the Sabbath – like visiting an elderly relative for Sunday lunch! Very nice, but one is glad when it's over and one can get on with one's life. Perhaps when the sea comes calling, God moves in and sits in the kitchen, or watches telly with the kids on the sofa.

My last poem, 'The Kingdom of Heaven', is one I wrote a number of years ago and is, as ever, about my experience of the omnipresence of the Divine:

> The Kingdom of God is within you:
> INSIDE
> At the core of your being
> Like a diamond in its box.
>
> The Kingdom of God is all around you:
> OUTSIDE,
> Like the air you breathe
> Or the wind that ruffles your hair
> On a summer's day.
>
> The kingdom of God is
> INVISIBLE
> Hidden from the eye like the song of a bird,
> Or the sound of panpipes
> In the thin mountain air.
> The Kingdom of God is HERE and NOW
> Plain for all the world to see
> If we only dare to LOOK.
>
> The Kingdom of Heaven may be likened
> To an earring dropped in a field.
> It lies hidden in the grass and you can
> Hunt all day and not find it.
> And then, when you've quite given up,
> There it is, laughing at you!
> The Kingdom of Heaven may be likened to a contact lens
> Lost down the bathroom waste.
> Without it, everything is blurred, grey, colourless,
> If you find it, the whole world shines
> Like stars on a frosty night.
> The Kingdom of Heaven may be likened
> To a wild creature, a squirrel or an urban fox.

One minute you see it, the next, you don't.
It is shy of strangers, wary of being trapped,
Caged and sold, freeze-dried
Or otherwise held to ransom.
The Kingdom of Heaven may be likened
To a great whale swimming in the sea.
It is vast, mysterious, scary;
Wild and untameable,
Too free by far to be contained
In even the largest net.
When it swims away we are desolate.
If it comes close, we are afraid.
We fear it will eat us alive for breakfast
And not even notice that we've gone.
Whoosh! And we'll be done for,
Swallowed whole, screaming for mercy.

The night of the whale's belly is dark,
Its walls smooth like glass.
There is no escape.
It is the end to running.
We sit in the dark, terrified,
Listening to the thud, the beat of our own heart.

Then, as our eyes grow accustomed to the dark,
We see a strange glow, a gentle light,
Like phosphorescence or the summer sea.
The whole world glows as if lit
By a thousand votive lights,
Floating on the dark surface of a lake
In a subterranean cave.

By this strange light we see,
For the first time
A twisted rope, a pulsating cord
That anchors us to the belly of the whale.

But after a while, perhaps a very long while,
It dawns on us that the twisted rope
Is not a fetter, but a lifeline.

For the Kingdom of Heaven may be likened
To the belly of a whale
In which we are held like a child,
Cushioned in the womb,
Awaiting the day of our birth
And the twisted rope which beats like a great artery
Is the mystical cord by which we are linked
To the heart of the Eternal God.

Part IV

Finding God in the Natural World

I caught this morning morning's minion, king-
   dom of daylight's dauphin, dapple-dawn-drawn Falcon, in his riding
   Of the rolling level underneath him steady air, and striding
High there, how he rung upon the rein of a wimpling wing
In his ecstasy! then off, off forth on swing,
   As a skate's heel sweeps smooth on a bow-bend: the hurl and gliding
   Rebuffed the big wind. My heart in hiding
Stirred for a bird,-the achieve of; the mastery of the thing!

                                                    Gerard Manley Hopkins

Chapter 13

This Planet Earth

The world is charged with the grandeur of God.
Gerard Manley Hopkins

I think I have always had a keen sense of wonder at the beauty of our world, although this has lain dormant sometimes when I have been deeply depressed. I have two separate memories of emerging from depression to see the beauty which surrounded me, and to which I had for so long been blind. The first memory is of walking through the park near my home and looking up to see the cherry blossom above me. In that moment I *saw* the flowers, as if for the first time, and was stopped in my tracks by their beauty. My heart somehow 'leaped' or 'swelled' within me as I experienced a joy that was not only emotional, but physical and spiritual as well. I can compare it to the epiphany (the showing forth) experienced by Irina Ratushinskaya when she was captivated by the sight of the 'upheaval of rainbow ice' on the window of her Siberian prison cell.

The second experience came later, on a day when I had managed to manipulate my long-suffering psychiatrist into giving me an urgent appointment, by dint of telling him that I had spent the early hours of that day sitting at the window of my attic flat contemplating throwing myself out of it. Having ascertained that I was not really a serious suicide risk, he asked me if I took any exercise. This was long before my dogs forced me out of doors twice a day, and I had to admit to being the couch potato that I then was. He shook his head sadly at me and told me that I must exercise and generate the endorphins, the brain chemicals, which would improve my mood. So, with exceeding ill grace, I took myself off to swim in the ice-cold sea.

It was not the temperature of the water that brought me to my senses, but a glimpse of the sunlight on the surface of the water as a windsurfer went scudding by. What is it about light that has this amazing power to lift our spirits? The psychiatrists speak of SADS, the Seasonal Affective Depressive Syndrome, in which some people find themselves beset by low spirits and negative thoughts in the dark days of winter. They have even invented electric light boxes which stimulate the brain and prevent the descent into winter blues.

Light has always been a potent symbol of the Divine, from the primitive peoples who worshipped the sun to the candle-lighters of our own day. T. S. Eliot writes wonderfully about the spiritual nature of light, whose 'eastern light our spires touch at morning', and which 'slants upon our western doors at evening', in *The Rock*:

> O Light Invisible, we praise Thee!
> Too bright for mortal vision.

It is not just the Christians, of course, whose worship is linked with the light, for lanterns are carried and candles lit at Diwali and a myriad of other festivals. My atheist critics will mutter 'Rubbish!', of course, and say that all this proves nothing except that humankind is drawn to the light because of some construct of the brain. Likewise, they will ask what the beauty of the Universe has to do with a Divine Power.

As I have noted earlier, there are also some deeply religious people who will worry that I am straying from the Gospel path to the worship of nature.

I have read that Hopkins himself was tormented by the thought that his love of the natural world and of the beautiful was separating him from God. He took comfort in the teaching of the medieval philosopher, Duns Scotus, who taught that 'the material world was a sacramental symbol of God, not something separate from him', but his Jesuit superiors remained sceptical at the time.

For me, the natural world is an amazing source of spiritual delight; a true manifestation of the Divine. It's not just that I think there is a power behind the Universe, a Divine being who created and is creating our world, but I believe that this Creator reveals himself/herself in the Creation.

This is what I understand by revelation, or epiphany. As Hopkins writes:

> The world is charged with the grandeur of God
> It will flame out, like shining from shook foil;
> It gathers to a greatness like the ooze of oil
> Crushed.

What powerful images Hopkins uses here; I am particularly fascinated by his use of 'the ooze of oil', which calls to mind the swell of the sea or the merciless flow of lava as it issues from an erupting volcano. Here we are, evoking the terrifying power of nature, or our world. The avalanche, the earthquake, the tsunami and the tornado.

As I write these words I am fascinated, as was Hopkins, by the incredibly diverse phenomena which make some of us aware of what I call The Divine. Already we have looked at the evocative power of fire and light, but we can be moved to worship and wonder as easily by a baby's smile as by the crashing of the waves on the beach.

So how does this finding God in all things natural affect me personally, in my life and relationship with God? The answer is complex, but I think that it hinges on the sense of wonder that is evoked by more and more things as I grow older. It is also very closely linked to the increased leisure provided by my retirement years. I am lucky enough to live by the sea, and each day my two dogs and I walk down the hill to the park and then along the sea's edge to a small café run by an enterprising ex-pilot named Chris. Here I buy my cappuccino, and the dogs and I descend to sea level to sit on the rocks at the edge of the water.

If the tide is right and the weather warm, the dogs walk out into the sea until the water laps around their shoulders; but they do not choose to swim. Instead, they lie or roll on the seaweed, or sit like the lions of Trafalgar Square on the edge of the small stone pier where the bravest of the locals swim, and the 'Devon Belle' docks to collect tourists for a tour of the harbour and Plymouth's great warships. It is here, sitting by the sea, that I feel closest to God.

Why, I wonder, do I experience this sense of closeness to the Divine here, rather than elsewhere? My guess is that it is part of the phenomenon of awe that so many feel in the face of power and mystery. Mountains make me feel the same way, and I expect that the desert would too. When I was in Chile, I would spend the day after hospital night duty at a Benedictine monastery in the hills outside of Santiago city. I would sit for hours, gazing at the outline of the great Andes mountains, which came into vision and then disappeared as the clouds moved across the sky.

I think that these mountains spoke to me even more powerfully of God than does the sea; for their appearance and disappearance mirrored my experience of the felt presence and absence of the Divine.

> I kiss my hand
> To the stars, lovely-asunder
> Starlight, wafting him out of it; and
> Glow, glory in thunder;
> Kiss my hand to the dappled-with-damson west:
> Since, tho' he is under the world's splendour and wonder,
> His mystery must be instressed, stressed;
> For I greet him the days I meet him, and bless when I understand.
> 'The Wreck of the Deutschland', by Gerard Manley Hopkins

God is not only to be found in storm and mountain, but in many secret places. As Hopkins says, 'there lives the dearest freshness, deep down things' (God's Grandeur'). And Blake encourages us to:

> To see a World in a Grain of Sand
> And a Heaven in a Wild Flower,
> Hold Infinity in the palm of your hand
> And Eternity in an hour.
> 'Auguries of Innocence', by William Blake

I am yet to have seen the world in a grain of sand, but the sight of heaven in a wild flower is a daily enchantment. Down by the sea, near where I live, we have two parks, a larger one with all kinds of tropical plants and sturdy trees, and a smaller, scruffier one, where the wild flowers grow. The first has been lately reserved for children (and dogs, which are tolerated only on a leash, lest they defile the grass), but the second is a free space where beasts may scamper and roll. This year, in Devon, we have had a magical spring and I have been enjoying a passionate love affair with the poppies.

First came the scarlet oriental poppies, standing proudly on their furry stems. There were eight of them, and I visited them every morning to mark their progress and gaze into their dark, mysterious hearts, where the black contrasted boldly with the red. There was a terrible day, when I saw that one flower had been broken from its stem (no doubt by a fellow poppy-lover), and I was filled with sadness and indignation.

When the eastern poppies were dead and gone, and seed-rich heads decapitated by some passing vandal, there was an interlude before the wild poppies appeared. They sheltered in the long grass which bordered the wire-enclosed tennis courts, their delicate vermilion and orange petals dancing in the wind. One morning, to my horror, the council gardeners appeared with an edge-cutter and began to cut down all the vegetation just outside the tennis court, including my poppies.

I rushed across and besought the man to stop, but he was not moved by my entreaties and muttered that they had to go because 'Health and Safety regulations decreed that they were a danger to the tennis players'! Eventually they made me sign a piece of paper to confirm that I had objected to the removal of the flowers! I am still waiting for a letter from the head of the city council, admonishing me for interfering in park maintenance.

Enough of the poppies! There were also the buttercups: golden and gleaming in the sunshine. No wonder Hopkins wrote 'Nothing is so beautiful as Spring'! Let me give you a taste of the poem:

Nothing is so beautiful as Spring –
When weeds, in wheels, shooting long and lovely and lush;
Thrush's eggs look little low heavens, and thrush
Through the echoing timbers does so rinse and wring
The ear, it strikes like lightening to hear him sing;

The best of the buttercups, however, grew between the cobbles of the private road that borders Elliot Terrace, where the Lord Mayor lives. Its survival, in the hard, dry earth, was for me a symbol of hope, of the magical persistence of life against all the odds.

It is clear that this life of contemplation, this flower-gazing, requires a degree of 'holy leisure'. My dogs and I are slow walkers by nature, so we are lucky that we have plenty of time to seek out the secret territorial messages of our furry brothers and any flowers that happen to be lurking in unexpected places. All three of us, however, have a special antenna for any hidden members of the feline species; the dogs, because of the thrill of the chase, and me, for fear of being pulled flat on my face yet again! My most ignominious tumble happened right outside the Lord Mayor's house just before Christmas a few years back, when I broke two of my front teeth on the cobbles. On another occasion, Mollie espied a squirrel by the roadside and the two of them led me a merry dance until her prey managed to scale the rough surface of one of the houses near where I live. There the four of us remained; the terrified squirrel spread-eagled on the wall, the dogs trying to reach it and me whimpering with exhaustion as I tried to pull over sixty kilos of wild dog down the road to the safety of my flat!

Enough of the spiritual delights of dog walking in Plymouth Hoe! Let us retreat safely inside my apartment and collapse in front of the telly. I have to admit here and now that, not only am I a shopaholic for clothes and *objets d'art* of all kinds, but I am also an avid watcher of television. In addition to crime and medical dramas and property searches, which I watch in the evening to 'chill out', as my young friends put it, I watch an amazing variety of wildlife programmes, which I see as a deeply spiritual activity.

If you consider yourself as a 'spiritual person', and are convinced that watching television is a vulgar waste of time, I entreat you to reconsider! (I am talking here about British television, not, alas, about the medium in the USA, for which I have little time.)

I have heard that David Attenborough, the father of wildlife television in the UK, is an unbeliever, but I find his knowledge of, and reverence for, our world and its creatures positively holy. From him, I have learned so many wonderful secrets of the planet, gleaned by the skilled and patient cameramen under his direction. With him, I have travelled to China to see the pandas, to the Galapagos Islands to observe the giant and ancient tortoises and to the Antarctic to marvel at the polar bears and penguins. David and his silent team can surely answer many of the questions with which Yahweh baffled the bemused and leprous Job:

> Do you know how mountain goats give birth?
> Or have you ever watched their hinds in labour?
> How many months do they carry their young?
> At what time do they give birth?
> Who gave the wild donkey his freedom,
> And untied the rope from his proud neck?
>
> Can the wing of the ostrich be compared
> With the plumage of the stork or falcon
> She leaves her eggs on the ground
> With only the earth to warm them;
> Forgetting that a foot may tread on them
> Or a wild beast may crush them.

Job 39:1–2, 5, 13–15

As I transcribe these words from my Bible, I am filled with wonder, not only at the writer's curiosity and his knowledge, but at how unbelievably privileged we twenty-first century people are to live in an age of the digital camera and the long distance lens. I thank God too for the amazing tiny cameras which are inserted into the private spaces of bird and beast, so that we may marvel at life in the meerkat's burrow, gasp with delight as a mother robin feeds her young, and weep with anguish as a hawk kills a rabbit or a cuckoo turfs the young owners out of their usurped nest.

Each spring and autumn, the BBC produces two entrancing series of programmes, entitled *Springwatch* and *Autumnwatch*. Hosted by two delightfully irreverent wildlife experts, it offers a grandstand view of British flora and fauna as they emerge from the torpor of winter to the glorious fecundity of spring. We see swallows return from their travels to nest under the eaves, and the young badgers frolicking with their fellow cubs. Each daily programme ends with a cliff-hanger: will the lone chick fallen from the nest survive and what will happen to the crazy bird that has built her nest on the back of a tractor?

Perhaps some readers will dismiss these ramblings as pure sentimentality, but I believe that such glimpses of the covert life with which we share the planet are truly an epiphany, a showing forth of the Divine. Perhaps the gentle men and women who share with us their wonder at the mystery of life are members of a special new priesthood which has no call to be either celibate or solemn, just to trade with the gifts that God has given them. As Hilda of Whitby, a seventh-century nun, exhorted her Sisters:

> Trade with the gifts that God has given you. Bend your minds to
> Holy Learning that you may escape the fretting moth of
> littleness of mind that would wear out your souls. Brace your
> will to action that you may not be the spoil of weak desires.
> Raise your heart and lapse in song which gives courage to the
> soul. Being buffeted by trials, learn to laugh. Being rebuked, give
> thanks, and having failed, determine to succeed.

After writing about *Springwatch*, I see Hilda's words in a new light. How can study of the life and ways of the wild things not be as holy a branch of learning as theology? As I listen to the dawn chorus here in Maine, USA, where I am writing this chapter, am I not hearing the birds in the wood gathering their courage to face a day of foraging, mating and feeding their young? Though I have to admit that the kookaburra is the only bird I know which laughs, the little birds on *Springwatch* are most certainly buffeted by many trials. Perhaps we have more in common with the creatures than we like to admit.

Chapter 14

Living with Creatures

There is sorrow enough in the natural way
From men and women to fill our day;
And when we are certain of sorrow in store,
Why do we always arrange for more?
Brothers and sisters, I bid you beware
Of giving your heart to a dog to tear.
    'The Power of the Dog', by Rudyard Kipling

The American priest writer, Andrew Greeley, in addition to his many novels, wrote a number of serious books. About twenty years ago, I stumbled on his book about myths, and was captivated by his description of the early desert nomads of Palestine as having two sorts, or classes, of god: their household gods, who protected and comforted them, and the infinitely mysterious and scary all-powerful God of the Mountain, El Shaddai. It seems likely that the transition to monotheism, the worship of a single deity, was a gradual one, for the need for tangible household gods is a human trait, and not easily satisfied by belief in the unseen God. In the Old Testament, Zophar of Naamath (whoever he was) asked Job:

Can you claim to grasp the mystery of God,
to understand the perfection of Shaddai?
It is higher than the heavens: what can you do?
It is deeper than Sheol: what can you know?
Its length is longer than the earth,
Its breadth is broader than the sea.
If he passes, who can stop him,
or make him yield once he has seized?
For he detects the worthlessness in man,
he sees iniquity and marks it well.
And so the idiot grows wise,
Thus a young wild donkey becomes tame.
               Job 11:7–12

El Shaddai is not exactly the kind of God a man would create to comfort himself, but more like the image conjured up by a man sheltering from a tornado, or clinging to his roof during a Bangladesh-style flood. It is not surprising, therefore, that humankind clings to its pictures of the Sacred Heart, its statues of the Virgin and even to its teddy bears. I have to admit that I used one or more of my teddy bears as companions and protectors until just a few years ago.

Such objects are recognised by the psychotherapists as 'transitional objects', something that links the child, or, indeed, the adult, with the security of home. The parents among you will recognise the phenomena of the 'blanky', the embarrassingly-grubby, well-sucked fragment of blanket or towelling without which a child is inconsolable.

In the last ten years of my hospital career, I took a large, rather floppy bear called Gus to work with me everyday. I would take him with me when I went to the wards to visit patients, walking shamelessly through the hospital corridors carrying him proudly for all to see. The consultants may have thought I was mad, and may have mocked me behind my back, but the patients loved him and would sit and hug him tightly as they talked to me of their hopes and fears, and their inevitable if not impending death.

There was one particular incident, when I admitted to the ward an outpatient – a very depressed woman with recurrent breast cancer, whom I felt was not well enough for the long drive home and who had no close support when she got there. At around half past ten that night, I received a call from the hospital to tell me that my patient was very distressed and insisting on going home. There was nothing for it but to return to the hospital, and Gus and I groaned as we made our way from my flat down the seventy-odd steps to the car.

When I got to the hospital, I sat beside the bed and Gus sat on it while we talked through Jane's feelings of fear, sadness, anger and despair. Eventually, I suggested that I leave Gus to look after her for me that night. At which point, she grabbed him and disappeared under the bedclothes, with Gus clasped to her bosom. Next morning they were still hidden under the bedclothes, but in better shape when they emerged. It was then that I decided that it would be wrong to part them, and suggested that Gus should accompany her home for a while to look after her. She accepted gratefully and that was how Gus went to Marazion in Cornwall for a week's support duty. The following week, he returned to Plymouth in a brown paper parcel and spent a lonely weekend in the hospital post room before we were reunited on the Monday!

Gus continued his hospital career alongside mine until we retired in August 2002. Like me, he still works from home (when I have a particularly distressed psychotherapy client), but mostly he sits on the back of the sofa, waiting for the next trip away from home when his services as companion and comforter will be required once more. The sad truth (for Gus) is that he has been well and truly supplanted in my affections by two large woolly dogs with bear-like faces, my beloved Mollie and Anka.

When I was a child, my mother always had one or two Cairn Terriers with which she was totally besotted. I knew, even then, that she loved the dogs more than me, and now I can understand why! I used to feel quite peevish about this, and when I was a young doctor I rather despised her preoccupation with her pets. Oh, the arrogance of my young self! Little did I know that when she died, her dog-worshipping spirit would take up residence in my own intellectual, religiously well-ordered soul!

Now, in my seventies, I become more like my mother every day: untidy, colourful, wildly creative and totally obsessed with my dogs! The thoughts that follow will be about finding God in my furry friends, so if this irritates you, please move on to the next chapter. Remember, however, that DOG is an anagram of GOD!

It is my firm belief that Chows are not only extremely beautiful, and completely enchanting, but also quite different from your average domestic pooch. I have become convinced of this not only by constant observation of their behaviour, but by the reading, some years ago, of two books, *King Solomon's Ring* and *Man Meets Dog*, by the then-renowned Austrian ethnologist (animal behaviourist), Konrad Lorenz. It was Lorenz's belief that there were two different types of dog: those who were descended from the jackal – Labradors, Retrievers, Collies, and so on – and a smaller, elite group of 'Spitz' dogs, which are descended from the wolf. This group includes the Chow, the Husky, the Keeshond, the Samoyed and a more recent species, the Alaskan Malamute. Most of these dogs, including the Chow, are characterised by short, alert ears, a thick coat and a curly tail. Lorenz believed that the Chow was the product of a union between the jackal and the Arctic wolf – a thought which delights my imagination.

In more recent years, the experts seem to believe that all dogs are descended from the wolf, although some are convinced that the Chow includes the bear amongst its ancestors. Whatever their origins, Chows are intriguing animals. The pet books describe them as aloof and condescending, one-man dogs, with a passionate loyalty to their masters. Lorenz describes how he bought a Chow puppy for his wife as a birthday present and kept it hidden for about a week until the right day, only to discover that the dog had bonded with him so strongly that it had no interest in its rightful owner.

Lorenz told this story in the context of a discussion on the phenomena of 'imprinting', in which certain birds, ducks and geese in particular, will bond with the first creature they see when they are hatched. Lorenz drew enchanting pictures of a group of baby goslings following him in solemn, single file because they were convinced he was their mother!

He collaborated with the English psychotherapist and doctor, John Bowlby, in an attempt to understand the process by which newborn creatures 'bond' with their parents, especially the mother. Bowlby described this process of bonding between mother and baby as 'attachment', and saw it as 'hardwired' – a natural mechanism in the brain that had developed for the survival of the infant. If you think about human behaviour for a moment, you will realise that most mothers are devoted to their young and would gladly give their lives for them. (How hard it is to comprehend what happens to those parents who abuse and even kill their children.)

As a therapist, I am constantly aware of the impact of the quality of maternal attachment on both men and women. Those children who have had a 'secure' attachment experience – their mothers have been 'attuned' to their needs, or, in common parlance, 'there for me' – are destined to become happy, confident adults who will mother their own children well when the time comes. In contrast, those children whose maternal care has been abusive or neglectful are far more likely to suffer from anxiety and depression, will be more inclined to choose an abusive partner and are likely to be inadequate mothers. There was a key research project by Harry Harlow, in which baby monkeys were removed from their mothers for variable periods of time. Those monkeys which were removed at birth had virtually no mothering skills when they themselves had offspring.

There are, of course, other circumstances which impact on the psychological growth of a child: maternal sickness, depression or bereavement, to quote but three. Bowlby and his colleague Robertson filmed the distress of a child left alone in hospital, as was then the custom. The impact it had on the doctors who saw this film led to the now familiar custom of mothers staying with their small children when they are admitted to hospital.

If you are wondering what this rather didactic digression has to do with God and dogs, let me make myself clear. Humankind, and, indeed, all creatures, are so wondrously made that the more we understand their functioning, the more we are moved to marvel at their Creator. I have no problem with Darwinian theory, for I see it as the Creator's way of creating and all the more cause for wonder.

As a therapist, human behaviour is of infinite fascination to me and, as a dog owner, I observe my two companions with interest and delight. Anka, my male dog, spends much of his time at my side, often requiring that I scratch his back, something which clearly gives him great sensual pleasure. Sometimes, however, when I am busy in my kitchen, I am summoned by his peremptory bark, only to find that he wants nothing more or less than a cuddle! Luckily, I find it quite funny that he expects me to come to him rather than the reverse, in the same way that he will not come for his supper when called but expects his meal to be delivered to between his outstretched paws! You may think I am singularly stupid and my dogs dreadfully spoiled, but I am fascinated by the way this originally wild animal has adapted to sharing my life and home.

Mollie, the bitch, is truly bear-like in appearance and much more of a loner by disposition. While Anka often sits by my side, Mollie always places herself at a distance, truly the dog who walks by herself.

I didn't get Mollie until she was fourteen months old, just two weeks after I had had a bilateral mastectomy for breast cancer. The breeder and her owner who brought her to me were not at all certain she would settle. And, indeed, I am convinced that she did everything in her power to make herself unwelcome in my house so that I would send her home! In particular, she took to peeing on the beds and sofas, not, as someone suggested, by way of territorial marking, as this was a true bladder-full which soaked through bedspread, duvet and sheets to the mattress. I remember one night a friend was staying and we deliberately left making-up her bed until the last minute. Little did I realise that Mollie was watching us and, as we straightened the quilt, she leaped on the bed and emptied her bladder in the middle of it!

Clever as she is, Mollie was no match for me and, determined to keep her, I bought waterproof covers for all the vulnerable furniture and decided to wait her out. Sure enough, she eventually capitulated and has not soiled anything since. She still plays cat and mouse with me, however, apparently reading my mind when I decide to groom or bath her, and shooting off at high speed into the garden to hide in the bushes! I love both my dogs, but I love Mollie especially because she makes me laugh, and, even more, because she is so feral, so wild, and yet has deigned to live with me and, by some strange miracle, loves me more than I love myself.

Just as the dogs have become attached to me, so have I become bonded to them, and it distresses me enormously to leave them. Each year, I spend two weeks with friends here in Maine and I am plagued by sadness and anxiety as the day approaches for me to leave Mollie and Anka. It is now ten days since I left them and the sadness has worn off, but if I don't get a daily report on their well-being, I know I will become anxious and imagine the worst. Once again, in this natural functioning of the mind, we see the design of the Creator working to safeguard the young and vulnerable of the species.

Here in Maine, there are different species of funny beasts to tug at my heart-strings. My friend Clare's house is in the woods, and I am proud to have contributed to a large picture window, which looks out on to the lawn on the edge of the wood. Clare is a keen birdwatcher, and has strung a wire from porch to verandah to support a large bird feeder in front of the window. While she delights in the visits to the feeder of the red cardinal and a horde of little birds, brown and yellow, whose names I do not know, I wait anxiously for the squirrel which makes perilous leaps from the rail of the verandah onto the feeder. To Clare's irritation and my delight, the squirrel settles down happily to gorge himself on bird seed, while the birds wait patiently in the surrounding trees.

This year, there have been new visitors to the woods: a beautiful hawk and her baby. We feared for the squirrels and the chipmunks, until there was a breathtaking stand-off meeting between the hawk and a particularly reckless squirrel. The two faced each other at close quarters on the verandah and then the squirrel washed its whiskers and the hawk flew away. We all breathed a sigh of relief.

I have written in a previous book about installing first one, then two, parrots, and then a pair of gerbils and a family of chipmunks in my room at the hospital. Henrietta, the forerunner of the chipmunks, was a wild little beast, but she made herself completely at home in the room, spending much of the day eating sunflower seeds on a small window-sill garden and returning to her cage unbidden when the sun went down. One night I came to bed late and, to my great distress, Henrietta was not in her cage. I need not have worried, for, after a frantic search of the room, I noticed a small round hole in my bedspread. Fancying a change of nest, my wild companion had bored through the bedding and set up house in my mattress.

Henrietta lived with me for years, taking over my desk as her hibernation quarters: one drawer for a nest, a second for a grain store and a third as a toilet. When I moved out of the hospital quarters to share a house with my Chilean friend, Consuelo, Henrietta was hibernating, so we carefully transported her in my desk to our new home. Alas, however, by the time the spring came we had acquired Winston, Joshua and Jericho, the first of my Chows. When Henrietta emerged from her hibernation, the dogs did what dogs do: chased her, caught her and killed her. I remember being desolate, sitting in the ENT (Ear, Nose and Throat) cubicle of the Casualty department, which I was employed to run, sobbing my heart out before I could face the endless stream of patients waiting for me.

So: living with animals is, for me, a source of endless delight, and I quite refuse to believe that this has nothing to do with the Divine. God created me, Henrietta, the parrots and of course, the Chows. How can I not love him for it!

Back in the UK, I am blissfully reunited with my dogs and all is well: Anka sits beside me on the sofa while I drink my first tea of the day and 'say' (or, rather, not say) my prayers. The phone goes and it is my friend Martin – therapist, theologian and retired Anglican priest. As I tell him of my holiday and my theology of dogs, he, at heart a cat man, exhorts me not to forget the humble moggy as an instrument of divine revelation. So here is a weak excuse to introduce you to a wonderful verse by the eighteenth-century poet, Christopher Smart.

Richard Mabey, in an article accompanying the poem in a recent issue of *Resurgence* magazine, describes Smart as 'a jobbing journalist and small time poetaster'. It seems that in 1756, 'he fell ill with religious mania', and spent the next seven years in 'Mr Potter's Private Home for the Insane in Bethnal Green'. Smart's consideration of his cat Jeoffry emerges as a deliciously-lucid passage embedded in his 'extraordinary' work *Jubilate Agno*, which Mabey describes as 'a vast sprawling celebration of creation'. I give you the first few lines of 'For I will consider my Cat Jeoffry':

For I will consider my Cat Jeoffry.
For he is the servant of the Living God duly and daily serving him.
For at the first glance of the glory of God in the East he worships in his way.
For this is done by wreathing his body seven times round with elegant quickness.

For then he leaps up to catch the musk, which is the blessing of God upon his prayer.

For he rolls upon prank to work it in.

For having done duty and received blessing he begins to consider himself.

For this he performs in ten degrees.

For first he looks upon his forepaws to see if they are clean.

For secondly he kicks up behind to clear away there.

For thirdly he works it upon stretch with the forepaws extended.

For fourthly he sharpens his paws by wood.

For fifthly he washes himself.

For sixthly he rolls upon wash.

For seventhly he fleas himself, that he may not be interrupted upon the beat.

For eighthly he rubs himself against a post.

For ninthly he looks up for his instructions.

For tenthly he goes in quest of food.

For having consider'd God and himself he will consider his neighbour.

Perhaps I should go on to consider finding God in madness, but I think this will do!

Chapter 15

Where the Wild Things Play

There is the sea, vast and wide;
with its moving swarms past counting;
living things great and small.
The ships are moving there
and the monsters you made to play with.

Psalm 104:25–26

I have written long of my domestic menagerie, but I cannot leave the subject of animals without speaking of the awe and wonder provoked in me by the creatures of the wild. In addition to the British *Springwatch* and *Autumnwatch* programmes, the wildlife watchers and their cameramen bring to my television screen the most breathtaking footage of the life of wild animals. 'Living things great and small', we are introduced to them all; in their dens, with their babies, hunting for food and generally relaxing.

One of the most enchanting programmes of the last few years is called *Meerkat Manor*; it is made with the help of a Cambridge research team, who have been studying these creatures in their natural habitat in Africa's Kalahari Desert for the past ten years. Meerkats live in extended families and, like many human families, are ruled by a matriarch. The researchers put a radio collar around the necks of the lead females and are thus able to keep track of the group when it moves about. At the risk of anthropomorphising, I will describe a little of these creatures' lives that mirror our own in so many ways. My favourite matriarch was named 'Flower' by the filmmakers, and we studied her life week after fascinating week. We were given views of the greatly-pregnant Flower entering her burrow to give birth. With hidden cameras, we watched the day-by-day maturing of the cubs until they were resilient enough to be carried by the scruff of the neck out to the wider, more dangerous, world. We watched entranced, as the babies grew and acquired personalities of their own, cared for initially by a 'nanny' from the family, and then taken out with the grown-ups and adolescents to forage for grubs, insects and other delicacies. When the cubs were too small to go out, one of the adults was left behind to guard them. He or she would sit on a small hillock, in characteristic upright pose, scanning the horizon for the sign of predators or rival meerkats.

The rivalry between the different groups was intense and they were highly territorial, attacking any creature that dared invade their patch. Occasionally, when the group was at home, the rival team would be sighted; when that occurred, Flower would immediately set out to do battle. Tails erect, the others would charge in her wake, a formidable sight, despite the fact that meerkats are no bigger than squirrels!

In the last series, Flower, whom both viewers and narrator had come to love, grew old and lost some of her vigour. After coming into conflict with one of the enemy, she suffered fatal wounds and died. Even as we grieved for her, one of her daughters assumed leadership of the group and life resumed its normal rhythm of rising, grooming, foraging, fighting and wonderful sessions of relaxing in a sort of group hug, with much grooming and bonding.

Of all the wild animals on television, however, I am most enthralled by the tigers. In one series, the presenter was a delightful Indian tiger expert who led us, whispering, into a game reserve to meet up with the beasts, all of whom he knew by name. Tigers are just so beautiful. Awesome predators, they can fell their prey with a single blow, and yet they are the tenderest of mothers. We watched the cubs from their earliest, most vulnerable days, then, as they grew older, as mischievous youngsters pouncing on each other or their mother's tail.

The ancient psalmist makes no mention of tigers, but he waxes lyrical over God's care for lions:

> You made the moon to tell the seasons,
> The sun knows when to set:
> You bring darkness on, night falls,
> All the forest animals come out:
> Savage lions, roaring for their prey,
> Claiming their food from God.
>
> Psalm 104:19–21

I am always perplexed when some of my friends show no interest in these creatures, while I am filled with awe and a powerful sense of the Creator. I feel so grateful to the men and women who make such films. Their ingenuity is boundless and their patience mind-boggling

In his series, *Planet Earth*, David Attenborough devoted the final ten minutes of his allotted hour to explaining how the film was made. Cameras were placed in sawn-off tree stumps with a remote control engine, so that the animal to be filmed was unaware that he or she was under observation. When the animal moved, 'tree-cam' followed, waiting stealthily to capture an intimate shot.

One of the most moving of recent wildlife films took us to the frozen wastes of the Arctic, where we saw white Arctic foxes and, of course, the fabulously beautiful polar bears. The emerging of the mother bear from her den with one, or even two, new cubs, was a breathtaking sight, as was the recording of their journey across the ice in search of food. The presenters, of course, were at pains to remind us of the dangers of climate change that put the very lives of the bears in jeopardy. There was a distressing demonstration of how global warming is melting the polar ice-cap, in a film that showed the adult bear fall through ice which was too thin to hold her. After six or more months of hibernation and the care of her newborn cubs, the mother bear is desperate for food and, if her hunting ground vanishes, she too will die.

It is only in recent years that I have become aware of the fragility of this planet of which we are the sole custodians. How does the saying go? 'If a butterfly flaps its wings, the leaves of the trees move in the Amazon Rain Forest.' How hard it is to face the fact that it is my profligate use of domestic energy – for example, the boiling of more water than I need to make a cup of tea – which contributes to the phenomenon (about which we long to forget) of our use of fossil fuels overheating our world. We might as well be tree dwellers, blissfully sawing-off the branch on which we are sitting!

Another wonderful programme took its viewers into the mysterious heart of China. We saw the fabulous rock formations in Guilin and watched, enchanted, as a fisherman used his tame cormorant to catch the fish that feed his family. This co-operation between man and beast – falcons, horses, dogs and so many more – is something we take for granted, often blind to the miracle that makes it possible to tame a wild animal. My wayward and stubborn Chows are an ancient species. It is thought that they came down through Mongolia to China, where they were used as hunting dogs, and (I feel sick at the thought) for food. It is said that one Chinese emperor had a team of over a thousand Chows which he used for hunting. As I described earlier, my beautiful two dogs, which walk sedately on Plymouth's waterfront with me, transform instantly into ferocious hunters when they see a cat or a squirrel. The hunting gene is clearly dominant in this fascinating companion!

Wild China took its viewers to eight different regions of the country, but, like most animal lovers, I am a sucker for the Giant Panda. I love all bears, and marvel at the Latin American Spectacled Bear, and the wild grizzlies as they fish for salmon in the Canadian rivers. Oh! But the Panda is so lovely! China has learned to take care of its unique treasures, and the cameraman had to venture miles into wild country to catch even a glimpse of it. From the comfort of my armchair, I watched enchanted at the sight of this black and white teddy bear, devouring bamboo shoots and caring for its young. I have just bought a calendar with twelve photographs of the Panda in the wild, so I can indulge my delight in bears throughout the next year. I must admit that, these days, I feel more drawn to love and praise of God while watching these programmes than I do in church.

I am drawn, also, to the men and women who make these amazing films. There is gentleness, a rare humility about them, which, to me, makes them seem like a different kind of priest: a minister of the spiritual, rather than of religion.

When I set out to write this chapter, my friends had booked us onto a 'whale-watching cruise', starting out from the city of Portland, Maine. We awoke in great excitement, sure that we would see at least one whale, and drove to the port whence the boat was to depart. As we approached the dock, however, the mist which was around when we woke became a dense fog. Ever optimistic, the cruise skipper took our forty dollars and set off in search of whales, reassuring us that some of his best sightings had been on days like this. The fog could lift at any moment, he protested, and, infinitely gullible, we believed him. After two hours, however, when we were way out of sight of land, he admitted that the chances of a sighting were slim. We sat on the top deck, anxiously scanning the sea, but saw only mirages of land and one lone petrel.

At first this seemed to be a totally abortive trip: forty dollars and five precious hours wasted. But, as always in adversity, I learned something important. Catharine McKenty, an Irish-Canadian friend of my hostess Clare, was staying with us in Maine. Catharine is finishing a book about her Aunt Polly, a great aunt who travelled by sea from Ireland to Canada in 1847, at the time of the potato famine. Interested in these brave people, many of whose children died on the voyage, I bought a book which told the story of a boy who had embarked in my home town of Plymouth for the Americas more than two hundred years before Catharine's Aunt Polly. *The Journal of Jasper Jonathan Pierce*, by Ann Rinaldi, begins on 6 September 1620. On the 16 September, Jonathan wrote:

> When this ship slipped her hawsers and sailed from Plymouth on September 6th, I left my brother Tom behind on the wharf. Tom, the other part of me. The younger, yet wiser. On the streets of London it was Tom who kept us alive. Tom who learned how to beg or steal food. How to stay warm. How to find work, and when we could not, how to pick pockets ... How can I live without Tom?

On 24 September, he wrote to Tom:

> The ocean goes on forever. It is so strange to see nothing but water. It is frightening. What am I doing here? Where does this ship take me? Will I ever see you again?

On 27 October, Jasper wrote of a storm at sea:

> When the first of it came the sea looked like a mad dog, foaming at the mouth ... The ship shuddered every time a wave poured over the decks. It was dark as night outside, though still mid afternoon ... The ship groaned like it would break in half.

Although this book is a work of fiction, the writer, like Catharine, has researched the documents of the day, and the events and characters portrayed are based upon real people. It was, however, only when we were at sea searching for whales in the fog that I realised something of what it must have been like for Catharine's Aunt Polly and those people upon whom 'Jasper' was based. On our trip, the fog was so dense that we couldn't see the lighthouses and the islands as we left Portland Harbour. For over four hours we could see nothing but sea, and grey, cold, impenetrable fog. It was not rough by mariners' standards but to us landlubbers it felt quite scary. It was during this cruise that I gained some insight into the dreariness and despair that must have afflicted those sailing to America or Australia. I had never given a moment's thought to my paternal grandfather Faeris, who emigrated to Australia around the same time as 'Aunt Polly'. How terrifying and bewildering it must have been for those young migrants, especially when a member of their family (like Polly's sister) died at sea. We are so used to radar and electronic direction finders that many of us forget the terror of being out of sight and reach of dry land. Once again, I thank God that I live in the twenty-first century and not in the sixteen-hundreds.

The other thought which occurred to me in this context of encountering the Divine beyond church boundaries, was how often it is that God is hidden from us as if in a fog. Cardinal John Henry Newman, when he was an Anglican priest and writer in 1833, wrote his famous hymn 'Lead Kindly Light' in one of those barren moments when God could be neither seen nor felt:

> Lead, kindly light, amid the encircling gloom.
> Lead Thou me on!
> The night is dark, and I am far from home.
> Lead Thou me on!
> Keep Thou my feet; I do not ask to see
> The distant scene; one step enough for me.

Uncertain that my memory of the hymn served me well, I asked Clare to find the words for me. To my delight, she came up not only with the text but this fascinating nugget of information: Newman was becalmed at sea when he wrote this hymn! As a young priest, John Newman became sick while in Italy and was unable to travel for almost three weeks. In his own words:

> Before starting from my inn, I sat down and began to sob
> bitterly. My servant, who had acted as my nurse, asked what
> ailed me. I could only answer, 'I have work to do in England'. I
> was aching to get home, yet for want of a vessel I was kept at
> Palermo for three weeks. I began to visit the churches, and they
> calmed my impatience, though I did not attend any services. At
> last I got off in an orange boat, bound for Marseilles. We were
> becalmed (this was, of course, a sailing vessel) for a whole week
> in the Straits of Bonifacio, and it was there I wrote the lines for,
> Lead Kindly Light, which have since become so well known.

Google threw in another jewel of information: Lead Kindly Light was sung by a soloist on the RMS Titanic, during a hymn-singing gathering led by the Rev Ernest C. Carter, shortly before the ocean liner struck an iceberg on 14 April 1912.

In the third verse of the hymn, Newman wrote:

> So long Thy power hath blest me, sure it still
> Will lead me on,
> O'er moor and fen, o'er crag and torrent, till
> The night is gone;
> And with the morn those angel faces smile
> Which I have loved long since, and lost awhile.

Although I am very familiar with 'Lead Kindly Light', I have never really asked myself what Newman meant by the 'angel faces'. As a celibate priest he could not be referring to his children, and the language would be excessive for friends, parishioners or colleagues. My first thought was that he was referring to life after death, but now I wonder if he was speaking of what is known as 'consolation' in prayer. It is very probable that he found it difficult to pray while he was ill, and also during the seemingly interminable wait for a ship to take him home. It may well be that he was clinically depressed, which would fit in with his 'dark night' and sense of 'encircling gloom'. Whatever the truth of this, the hymn is much loved and clearly echoes the experiences of many people.

I must admit that I was fascinated by the irony that the pious group on the Titanic sang this hymn before, rather than during, the terror and chaos that followed with the break-up of the world's proudest and newest steam ship. I'm glad I don't have to comment on this coincidence for a theology paper!

It was in my eighteen months living in the grounds of Ampleforth Abbey that I learned that God's 'absences' are as important as his presence. There is a quotation, which I believe comes from the works of the Prophet Mohammed (Peace be upon Him), which says: 'God is as near as the neck of your camel.' Another image that I was given is that God can be so close that one cannot see him, like having a cloth over one's face or being blindfold, or, indeed, in a fog. I was taught that any man or woman who embarks upon a life of prayer in 'pursuit' of the Divine will experience times of desolation, when God seems to have abandoned them; as well as times when he is felt to be vibrantly, wonderfully, close. It is tempting to believe that, if we can no longer 'find' God, it is because we have sinned or displeased him or her in some way. That this is a false premise is shown most clearly in the lives of the Saints. It is said that the 'great' St Teresa of Avila, the feisty sixteenth-century Carmelite nun, received no 'consolation' in prayer for over twenty years. It is quoted of her that she said to God, in a peevish moment (her carriage, I think, had overturned on a muddy road), 'Lord, if this is how you treat your friends, it is no wonder you have so few of them'!

As you will, of course, realise, I never saw the whales, and the chance to write ecstatically at first hand of the 'monsters' God made to play with was denied me! I have, however, seen so many whales, sharks and cavorting dolphins on my television screen that I could have written with passion of the magical sight of this great beast of the seas surfacing with a spouting of sea water and then diving again with a thunderous slap of its tail on the water.

Here endeth my account of experience of the Wild Things at play, and I can only commend these wonderful programmes to anyone who wishes to pursue the Divine beyond the boundaries of their parish church.

Chapter 16

God and the Tsunami

Who pent up the sea behind closed doors
When it leapt tumultuous out of the womb?

Job 38:8

On Boxing Day 2004, the lovely coast of Southern Thailand was hit by a natural disaster, the proportions of which shocked the world. Somewhere deep in the Indian Ocean, the earth moved; tectonic plates shifted, resulting in an enormous and terrifying wave which swept silently inland, engulfing men, women and children alike, smashing luxury villas and fishermen's boats with equal ferocity. It swept inland for a distance of three kilometres, overpowering the thousands of desperate people in its path.

The tsunami was 'special' because, as natural disasters go, it was both rare and spectacular; we are used to hundreds dying in earthquakes and floods, but these usually happen to 'others', to the poor of Bangladesh or Afghanistan. Thailand was different because it was packed with western holidaymakers: *our* sons and daughters, relatives and friends, holidaying in resorts familiar to us, if only by name.

It is not my purpose here to ask why we care more about our own than 'foreigners', but to ask the impossible, unanswerable question: Where was God that Boxing Day? How can you and I, and people less educated than ourselves, continue to believe in a loving, all-powerful Creator God in the face of such devastation? The questions which occur to me are these:

Did God deliberately cause the tsunami? Did he make it happen?

Did God know it was going to happen and, if so, why didn't he stop it?

Is God as powerless as us in the face of natural disaster?

Does God *care* when lives are smashed, little children torn apart, faces burned beyond recognition?

My Novice Mistress once said that I asked the wrong questions, but I think we all have a God-given right to ask any question that occurs to us. What we must understand, however, is that some questions have no answers. Oh, you will find people – priests and lay people, gurus and wise men – who think they have all the answers. Some will say that the tsunami was God's punishment for the moral corruption of the holiday-makers. Others will insist that although God created the world, she does not interfere in it. This, I think, is called the theology of the Watchmaker God: she makes the world, winds it up and leaves it to run on its own. My hunch is that there's a grain of truth in that, because I surely don't believe in a punishing God wreaking havoc on her people (whatever the Old Testament may say to the contrary).

If God is all-powerful, and that is my intuition, why doesn't she intervene to save her people? After all, the God of the Old Testament held back the Red Sea so that the Israelites might cross unharmed. I don't know; and neither does anyone. The answer to all this is that we have to learn to live with the mystery. Some 'natural' disasters seem to have man-made roots. Desperate people clear land to grow food, and the rain rushes down the bare hillside and carries them and their houses away. Greedy loggers clear the Amazon, greenhouse gases accumulate and polar bears face extinction. What a lot we have to learn, and do. I pray:

> Grant Lord that I may change the things I can change,
> Accept the things I cannot change
> And the wisdom to know the difference.

If we can accept that the ultimate spiritual *why* of most natural disasters is beyond our understanding, then we can learn to be comfortable with Mystery. In this context, it is worth reading the last two chapters of the Book of Job, the story of the archetypal '*good*' man struck low by God; in our times, Job would be the man who loses not only his job and savings, but also his wife and kids. Then, to add insult to injury, he becomes incurably ill with a singularly disgusting disease. First of all, Job's friends tell him he's being punished by God and Job protests he's done no wrong. Eventually, Job is driven to demand an explanation of the Divine only to get an earful about how little he knows:

> Then from the heart of the tempest Yahweh gave Job his answer.
> He said:
> 'Who is this obscuring my designs with his empty-headed words?

Brace yourself like a fighter,
Now it is my turn to ask questions
And yours to inform me.
Where were you when I laid the earth's foundation?
Tell me, since you are so well informed!
Who decided the dimensions of it, do you know?
Or who stretched the measuring line across it?
What supports its pillars at their bases?
Who laid its cornerstone
When all the stars of morning were singing with joy,
And the sons of God in chorus were chanting praise?
Who pent up the sea behind closed doors
When it leapt tumultuous out of the womb ...
Have you ever in your life given orders to the morning?
Or sent the dawn to its post,
To grasp the earth by its edges
And shake the wicked out of it?'

Job 38:1–13

I find these last few chapters of Job quite magical; not just for their poetry, but also for the image of the world they open up in my mind.

I feel the same sense of awe that I experience when watching wildlife films on television. My own sense of the Divine is nearly always accompanied by awe and wonder, whether it is aroused by snow-capped mountains, life in the womb, music or a particularly beautiful work of art.

Although I love the last few chapters of Job, and understand them as a challenge to Job's questioning of God, I do not interpret them as a message that God is not to be questioned. After all, what parent would forbid his or her child to ask questions? The right to ask, of course, does not carry with it the right to a truthful reply, because children, like grown-ups, are not always ready for, or equipped to deal with, a complicated answer. So the message which I take from Job is that we should feel free to question God when we feel he is acting unfairly.

Stuck in the front of my Book of Psalms I find, once more, the priest George Herbert's wonderful poem 'Bitter-Sweet':

Ah my dear angry Lord,
Since thou dost love, yet strike;
Cast down, yet help afford;
Sure I will do the like.

> I will complain, yet praise;
> I will bewail, approve:
> And all my sour-sweet days
> I will lament, and love.

This contrasting pattern of questioning and accepting the actions of the Divine seems to be at the heart of true faith, of an intimate relationship with God. It appears again and again in the psalms, as the poet demands to know why God has forsaken him and begs to be rescued:

> Lord listen to my prayer:
> Turn your ear to my appeal
> The enemy pursues my soul;
> He has crushed my life to the ground;
> He has made me dwell in darkness
> Like the dead long forgotten.
> Therefore my spirit fails,
> My heart is numb within me.
> Lord make haste and give me answer;
> For my spirit fails within me.
>
> Psalm 142: 1, 3–4, 7

While it feels legitimate to me to ask of God what on earth she thinks she's doing to us or those we love, there comes a time when the only peace to be found is in submission and acceptance. My own experience of imprisonment and solitary confinement in Chile was marked first by frantic prayer for my release, not unlike the 'prayer in desolation' of Psalm 162, but then I came to understand that the better way was to try to accept what was happening and, more difficult, what might happen in the future.

I have written in a previous book, *Audacity to Believe*, of how, in Chile, I was taken before the fiscal, the military prosecutor, who told me that I might be found guilty of killing the maid in the house where I was arrested, and, if so, would likely be sentenced to a long term in prison. In my mind, I fought with God all of one night and eventually was able to give in, to abandon myself to whatever God wanted of me.

At the time, this was an immensely powerful experience, and I came to understand the meaning and consequences of what is called *abandonment*. I was greatly helped by an anonymous poem on the subject from a book that had been given to me, *Disciples and Other Strangers* by E. J. Farrell:

Abandonment is managing nothing,
Blocking or blotting out nothing,
Expecting nothing.

Abandonment is receiving all things
The way
One receives
A gift
With opened hands,
And opened heart.

Abandonment to God
Is the climactic point in any man's life.

This experience has somehow shaped my response to life and, although I am in no way immune to fear and uncertainty, once I have regained my spiritual balance I am better able to cope than in my earlier years. I suppose facing the fact that I had cancer in both breasts in 2002 was one of the hardest things I have had to do, although, in hindsight, not as hard as losing my job at the hospice ten years earlier.

In these and other, lesser, disasters, I return again and again to Archbishop Helder Camara's wonderful poem 'Go Down Into the Plans of God', from his book, *The Desert is Fertile*, which includes the lines:

Simply do not be afraid
Let go. You will be led
Like a child whose mother
Holds him to her bosom
And against all comers is his shelter.

For those unfamiliar with Camara, I should explain that he was for many years Archbishop of the diocese of Olinda and Recife, in Brazil's impoverished North-east. He was a man of small stature with a feisty disposition and an enormous heart, who fought endlessly for the rights of his people against the oppressive powers of government. Here is the Archbishop challenging the God who should be caring for the poor and the homeless:

How can you bear to see these millions of your sons and
daughters living in subhuman conditions owing to the
selfishness and ambition of unjust and oppressive minorities?

No wonder the government hated him! He continues berating God:

> By now you must have realise that your cataclysms – floods,
> droughts, volcanic eruptions, typhoons, earthquakes – affect the
> little ones most of all, whose life is already subhuman.

Like Herbert before him, Camara laments and loves; 'Ah, my dear, angry
Lord,' we can hear him say.

There is a story told that, during the Second World War, some soldiers
entered a devastated French village and noted that the statue of Jesus in
the market place was missing both its arms. At the base of the statue there
was a note: 'I have no arms but yours'.

Herein, I believe, lies the answer to where we find God in natural
disasters. We should look, not for the archetypal, tyrannical, angry old
man of our Sunday School nightmares, but for the ordinary men and
women who, faced with appalling suffering, find within themselves the
wellsprings of Divine compassion. The Good Samaritan is alive and well
today, as are the brave professional nurses and healers. The Red Cross, the
Red Crescent, Oxfam, *Médecins Sans Frontières* and many others: all bear
the light of Christ into the darkness of disaster.

> I will hold the Christ-light for you
> In the night-time of your fear

My friend Sister Bridget Folkard, invalided out of Rwanda with a broken
arm, has just done a stint in Haiti, where the devastation of the January
2010 earthquake is still shattering lives. She writes:

> The earthquake affected over two million people. Some of the
> rubble has been cleared, and assessment is proceeding for some
> houses that are standing, but cracked, but in the main it is still a
> city of ruins, of tents and refuse, with contaminated waters
> exposing a fragile population to epidemics. Everyday we felt the
> impossibility of the situation, and everyday we also know that
> one can only do one thing for one person: treat the person
> before you with respect and humanity.

When Jesus washed his disciples' feet he was doing a role-play of what it means to be his disciple: he proclaimed it at the outset of his ministry when he quoted Isaiah 61:

> He has sent me to bring good news to the poor,
> To bind up hearts that are broken;
>
> Isaiah 61:1

And he demonstrated it at his farewell dinner. There was no word about celibacy or the evils of homosexuality; there was nothing about birth control, churchgoing or respect for bishops. No. He told us to love one another as he had loved us, and to care for each other's blisters and dirty feet. How is it, I wonder, that we have strayed so far from his core message?

Part V

Our Response to the Divine

Then I heard the voice of the Lord saying:
'Whom shall I send? Who will be our messenger?'
I answered, 'Here I am, send me'.

Isaiah 6:8-9

Chapter 17

Caring for the Planet

We can relate to our planet Earth in two ways: either we can act as tourists and look at the earth as a resource of goods and services for our use, pleasure and enjoyment, or, we can act as Earth Pilgrims and treat the planet with reverence and gratitude. Tourists value the earth and all her natural riches only in terms of usefulness to themselves. Pilgrims perceive the planet as sacred and recognise the intrinsic value of all life. The living Earth is good in itself with all its grace and beauty.

Sutish Kumar, *Resurgence* magazine 255 (July/Aug 2009)

I am embarrassed and ashamed to admit that it is only in very recent years that I have thought of this planet as my home which I share with you and the rest of God's creatures. I was about to write 'humankind' and then realised that I was making the very same mistake that so many good, religious people have made since time began: I was assuming that Man, in the generic sense, is the most important creature on the earth, more important than the animals in the forest, the fish in the sea and the birds of the air. More important, indeed, than the very earth upon which we depend.

How blind I was, and how arrogant, and yet I was brought up, like so many Christians, to take literally God's command to Noah after the flood:

> 'Be fruitful, multiply and fill the earth. Be the terror and dread of all the wild beasts and all the birds of heaven, of everything that crawls on the ground, and all the fish of the sea; they are handed over to you.'
>
> Genesis 9:1–2

Well, well! How very convenient for mankind: a God given mandate to shoot tigers for their skins, bash seal cubs to death on the ice and chase foxes until they are terrified and exhausted, then set the dogs on them. I find it hard to reconcile this passage with the account of God's creation of the earth; you will find this in the first chapter of the book of Genesis, but let me give you a flavour of it:

> In the beginning God created the heavens and the earth. Now the earth was a formless void, there was darkness over the deep, and God's spirit hovered over the water.
>
> God said, 'Let there be light'. God saw that light was good, and God divided light from darkness. God called the light 'day' and the darkness he called 'night'. Evening came and morning came: the first day.
>
> Genesis 1:1–5

The story goes on to tell how God created a vault to divide the sea from the heavens and then he made the land and he found it to be 'good'. Likewise, he made the plants:

> God said, 'Let the earth produce vegetation; seed bearing plants, and fruit trees bearing fruit with their seed inside, on the earth.' And so it was ... and God saw that it was good.
>
> Genesis 1:11–12

After God made the sun, the moon and the stars and set them in the vault of heaven, he saw that 'it was good'.

Then, as we know, came the fish in the sea and the birds of the air: all found to be very pleasing to their Maker.

On the sixth day, God said:

> 'Let the earth produce every kind of living creature: cattle, things which crawl (small mammals, reptiles, amphibians and insects) and every kind of wild beast.'
>
> Genesis 1:24

The dog that was to become man's companion, the horse that he would tame and ride and of course the cats, great and small, wild and friendly, the lions and tigers, the bears, brown, black and white and all the other wonderful creatures with whom we share the earth.

Lastly, of course, we know that God created man:

> God said, Let us make man in our own image, in the likeness of ourselves, and let them be masters of the fish of the sea, the birds of heaven, the cattle, all the wild beasts and all the reptiles that crawl upon the earth.
>
> Genesis 1:26

In the second chapter of Genesis there is another account of the creation which makes it clearer that friendship, rather than dominance, should be the relationship between man and creation:

> Yahweh God planted a garden in Eden which is in the East, and there he put the man he had fashioned ... He put him there in the Garden of Eden to cultivate and take care of it.
>
> Genesis 2:8–9

This second account of the creation is fascinating and I see it as key to understanding the right relationships between man and beast:

> Yahweh God said, 'It is not good that man should be alone. I will make him a helpmate.' So from the soil Yahweh God fashioned all the wild beasts and all the birds of heaven.
>
> Genesis 2:18–19

You know the end of the story: God created the first woman out of Adam's rib. We know too, that from the beginning, man felt himself to be superior to his helpmates: the animals, the birds, the woman Eve and those who came after her.

Now I, like most scientifically-aware people, do not take the Genesis myth literally. Sure, I believe that God created the earth, but there is ample evidence that the world was not made in seven days, but rather over millions of years. Like most scientists, I know and believe in the theory of Evolution: that simple, primitive creatures evolved into more complex ones. Darwin's theory is that the fittest of each species survived *because* they were able to change and adapt to their environment. Those that failed to adapt perished, and so it will be with 'man', with us, if we do not adapt and change our lifestyle in accordance with the needs of the planet on which we live.

Satish Kumar is an ecologist who, in his youth, was a Jain monk in India. As a young man he made a long pilgrimage, carrying no money so making himself dependent on the people he met. Satish eventually settled in the North of Devon, where he works to make others aware of how to live in a right relationship with the planet.

As editor of *Resurgence*, a journal bringing together ideas on spirituality and ecology, he wrote in a recent issue:

> Indigenous people of the world lived and behaved as pilgrims. The earth was their temple, their church and their mosque. They went into the wild for their vision quest, for their prayers and meditation. They did not look up to the sky to find heaven: their heaven was here on earth.

He goes on to speak of St Francis, whom many see as a prophetic figure in his love of the planet and all its creatures:

> St Francis was a pilgrim of this sacred planet. Wolves, birds and all other creatures were his kith and kin; the sun and the fire were his brothers: the moon, the stars, the wind and water were his sisters.

He articulates some of the truths that I have learned over the years, by listening to Clare and the wildlife programmes and by sitting at the sea's edge with my dogs. I now understand Satish when he writes, of his own religion:

> For Hindus, god is not a person sitting in paradise. For them, all life is imbued with the divine. Everything from the high Himalayas is permeated through and through with the Sacred spirit. Hindus are pilgrims on planet Earth.

Although, as a Christian, I have a personal God and believe in the life and light of Christ 'revealed' in the world around us, I feel very at home with the Hindu concept that everything is 'imbued with the Divine'. Once we believe this, our relationship with the earth can never be the same again.

As my friend Neil McKenty, a writer, broadcaster and ex-Jesuit, puts it: 'The earth is the face of God. When we ravage the earth we scar his face.'

The writing of this chapter has been interrupted by my return to the UK and the jetlag that followed it. It was a tiresome journey, marked by a nine-hour wait at Portland Airport and a miserable few hours on the floor at Newark, as we waited for the flight which was to replace the one we had missed. There was, however, a silver lining to the cloud; in that I had time to read most of a book on *Care for Creation* a 'Franciscan spirituality for the earth'. The book, published in 2008, is co-authored by a theologian, Ilai Delio, an ecologist, Douglas Warner and an art therapist and spiritual director, Pamela Wood. Both Delio and Warner are Franciscans, and I loved their approach to their subject.

I was, in particular, grateful for the chapters on ecology, for they helped my understanding of our dependence on the planet and the ways in which we are damaging it:

> A fundamental lesson to learn from ecology and an understanding of eco-systems is that:
> *every resource we need comes from somewhere*
> and
> *everything we throw away goes somewhere else.*
> Ilai Delio, Douglas Warner and Pamela Wood, *Care for Creation*
> (my italics)

It is not my intention to write a treatise on recycling, waste disposal or global warming; I clearly don't know enough to do that. *But*, I do know that the subject is crucially important and that I cannot be a decent human being, let alone a god-fearing one, without learning enough to alter my lifestyle and reduce my 'carbon foot-print' (the impact of my consumption and waste upon this earth). Father Thomas Berry, the American priest who did so much to raise Christian awareness of the link between spirituality and the ecology, puts it bluntly:

> The Human Community and the Natural World will go into the future as a single sacred community or we will both perish in the Desert.

What does it *mean*, then, to be a 'single sacred community' with the Natural World? What has this amazing, rather mystical concept got to do with recycling, low voltage electric light bulbs and what I have taken to calling my 'save the world' shopping bags (which I inevitably leave behind when I go to the supermarket!)?

If we go back to the simple concept of resources and waste, it's marginally easier to get a handle on it. Resources, presumably, are food, water, timber, oil, minerals, land, the animals and plants and, of course, the air we breathe and the earth we walk on. Thinking of the earth brings me to the mind-blowing *Chief Seattle's Testimony – An 1854 Oration*. Here is the beginning of it. You can get the rest from the amazing 'Mr Google'!:

> The great chief in Washington sends word that he wishes to buy our land.
> The great chief also sends us words of friendship and goodwill. This is kind of him since we know he has little need of our friendship in return.
> But we will consider your offer. For we know that if we do not sell, the white man may come with guns and take our land.
> How can you buy or sell the sky, the warmth of the land? The idea is strange to us. If we do not own the freshness of the air and the sparkle of the water, how can you buy them?
> Every part of this Earth is sacred to my people. Every shining pine needle, every sandy shore, every mist in the dark woods, every clearing, and the humming insect, is holy in the memory and experience of my people … We are part of the Earth and it is part of us.
>
> *Chief Seattle's Testimony – An 1854 Oration,* an excerpt of the full statement attributed to Chief Seattle, written by Ted Perry

Satish was right when he said that the indigenous people of the world behaved as pilgrims: the earth was their temple, their church and their mosque. Strangely enough, that is how I have come to feel: I am more peaceful and more centred on God by the sea than I was in my parish church. *Chief Seattle's Testimony* reads like scripture to me: how far we modern people have strayed from his basic intuition that all the world is holy ground and ours only in the sense that we have stewardship of it, that we are responsible for it during our lifetime.

My Franciscan book provided me with another powerful fact about our 'Mother Earth': the top soil which makes the earth fertile is eroding away, threatening the ability of future generations to grow their food:

> It takes centuries to form just an inch of topsoil, with microbes and micro-organisms working to break down rock and combine it with decaying material ... we are losing top soil to wind and water erosion far faster than it can be replaced.

In addition to this loss of topsoil:

> Industrial agriculture consumes water from underground aquifers faster than it can be recharged. Future generations will have less soil, fossil fuels and clean water than we do.

Rachel Carson, in her prophetic book *Silent Spring*, described the widespread pollution of our water sources with industrial chemicals, and laid the foundation in the 1980s for the emergence of the now familiar concept of 'sustainability', defined by *Our Common Future*, the United Nations World Commission on Environment and Development, as 'meeting the needs of the present without compromising the ability of future generations to meet their needs'.

This notion of sustainability raises, for me, the inevitable question of needs versus wants. When I came out of the convent in 1980, I was determined to be holier and more frugal than the nuns who had rejected me and so I set up my flat with Oxfam china and no curtains, no rugs and no electrical gadgets. The process by which I slowly acquired a television a washing machine and vacuum cleaner has been told before in *Sharing the Darkness*, but it made a good story at the time. It took me a while to learn that not everyone's needs are the same, and sometimes it is better to have the humility to admit one's needs rather than make oneself sick denying them.

Having said that, I, like most of my friends, have taken the first steps towards a greener lifestyle. By this, I mean that I recycle my glass, my plastic, paper and so on. I also use low energy light bulbs, though just where I am supposed to put the forty watt ones sent to me by my electricity provider I am not sure. As to my 'Save the World' shopping bags, I really do try, and when I forget them I use the plastic bags provided as dog poo bags (except the ones with 'Save the Baby' holes in, of course!). However, I do regularly fail to switch off the television standby light when I go to bed. I know it's stupid, but I am always too tired to remember, or, if I do remember, I'm in bed by then and can't face getting out.

Also, I had better admit it: I have central heating *and* a tumble dryer. I am old enough to remember the 1947 winter, when we had no heating and my parents' hot water bottle froze in their bed! I do try to limit my use of heating but my friend John sneaks it on when I'm not looking (because he is of the generation which has always had it!). The other thing is that my dogs are *always* on the wrong side of the French windows leading to the garden, so I have an evil tendency to leave the door open and heat the outside world! Another issue, of course, is using public transport, rather than the car. Oh dear: I still haven't got my bus pass, although I've been eligible for it for years. At the moment I am forced to walk more than usual because John has borrowed my car to go to work, since someone (perhaps a conservationist) sawed through his steering column and stole his steering wheel.

As you can see, I have a long way to go on the Conservation Path, but perhaps I deserve a few green stars for trying.

> Live simply that others may simply live.
> Mahatma Gandhi

It's a great motto, a good rule of life, and one which has recently been adopted by CAFOD, the charity Catholic Action for Overseas Development. Like our personal response to Climate Change, our attempts at living simply will vary according to our life situations. Time was when I lived in one room, and very happy I was too. Now, I live in a three-bedroom apartment which feels like a palace. No, it doesn't feel too big. It feels just right and I delight in sharing it with my friends and 'adopted children': by which I mean John, whom I feed in the evening, Joe and Monique, who use my washing machine *and* my tumble dryer (because theirs is broken and it seems too much to ask that they carry bin liners of wet washing up to their third floor flat). I also share it, of course, with my psychotherapy clients, whom I see in my living room, where I also paint, write, sew, knit, watch television and scratch the dogs' backs. That is how my life has developed and if it's more complex than simple, I'm not sure what I should do about it.

I go into all this, perhaps unnecessary, detail because it seems important to be real and truthful rather than give the impression that I have all these important issues sussed. The truth is, for the greater part of my life I have devoted my energies to caring for other people, and the hardest lesson I have had to learn is how to care for myself. Caring for the planet therefore, has only been on my agenda for the last few years.

I end this chapter with a verse from John Harriott's poem 'Our World'. It's a long quote but very beautiful:

Let us fix this world in our sight,
put our ear to it
and listen to its living sounds:
the roaring flame in its hearts core,
the rumble of rock and the rushing of waters.
The rhythm of the ocean, the crash of the avalanche;
the susurration of sand, the crumble of soil,
the pelting rain and the tumbling river.
Let us see the lark ascending, the stretching geese,
the sparrow in the park, the eagle on the mountain top.
Let us see the whale spouting,
the shoals of mackerel, the salmon leaping.
And the running deer, the thundering buffalo,
the patient elephant, the durable horse.
The worm in the ground, the butterfly upon the flower,
the spider in its web, the scorpion beneath the store:
the jackal, the vulture and the ravenous shark;
Let us see and listen to
the oceans, the pampas, the jungles and the desert.
Let us watch with wonder the sun's fire and the cold moon,
the light and the darkness,
the crackle of lightening and the thunder clouds,
the hurricane flaring and the wind from the warm south.
Let us love this world and revere it.
And God saw everything that he had made,
and behold, it was very good.

Chapter 18

Caring for One Another

There is room in the world for loving.
There is no room for hate.
'Our World', by John Harriott

I love the brevity and the clarity of these words by John Harriott. They are pure Gospel; a précis of Jesus' message, his teaching, his legacy. Being a Christian, a follower of Jesus-who-became-the-Christ, is about loving one another; it's all there in St John's Gospel, in the Last Supper discourse:

'My little children,' he said,
'I give you a new commandment: love one another;
just as I have loved you,
you also must love one another.
By this love you have for one another,
everyone will know that you are my disciples.'
John 13:34–35

These words are, for me, the most important in the scriptures: so why do Christians of all denominations forget them and get het-up about issues which are peripheral, if not completely irrelevant, to Jesus' message?

When I was a child, it was fish on Friday, or, rather, abstinence from meat, which distracted us. And then there was the wearing of hats: good Catholic women covered their heads in church because St Paul had decreed it two thousand years earlier. Nowadays, it is the notion of women priests, women bishops and the evils of homosexuality that obsess the theologians. What nonsense it all is! We and they, laity and

154

priests, should be exploring, discussing just what it means to love one another and how we can do it better, so that we can truly call ourselves Christian. We should admit, too, that Christianity as a religion has no monopoly on love, for the love of God and neighbour is at the heart of *all* the great religions.

I think it's worth, therefore, to spend a little time unpicking Jesus' words: trying to understand exactly what he meant. This seems to me an infinitely more profitable exercise than struggling to understand the Trinity, that mysterious concept that merges and separates the Triune God, the Father, the Son and the Holy Spirit. There are some mysteries that we must learn to live with, but the meaning of 'love one another' is not one of them, so I shall attempt to 'liberate' the meaning of this theology.

The first thing to say, I think, is that love is not a feeling. Loving friends and family is not about *being in* love, it is a way of *being with* or 'treating' some one. It is about respect for the other, about kindness, gentleness, sharing and empathy. It is about listening with undivided attention to what the other says, and struggling to understand what he or she is saying and where he or she is coming from. Love is also about humility; believing that the other person may be right, or in possession of more of the truth than we are. And if we still think we are right – for example, as I think I am right to believe in the ordination of women – then we must argue our case gently or accept that the other is not yet in a position to change his or her mind. There comes a point when one must agree to differ, to respect the other person's right to his or her view.

Important as is the way we are with people, it is even more important to acknowledge the other's God-given right to life, liberty and well-being, what we call their 'human rights'. The sociologist Abraham Maslow devised a Hierarchy of Human Needs, which is taught to all psychologists and social workers, and which I find useful for under-standing and teaching about emotional distress. It looks like this (see p. 156).

At the base of this triangle, underpinning all life, are our most primitive needs: food, water and shelter. When these needs are not met, we die. It's as simple as that. These are the needs which the aid agencies – OXFAM, Save the Children and the like – struggle to meet. Every time there is an earthquake, a flood or a volcanic eruption, these basic needs are put in jeopardy. Wars and terrorist attacks also leave people in desperate need, so that those who are able take what they can carry and

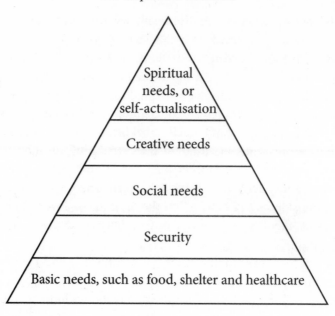

Spiritual needs, or self-actualisation

Creative needs

Social needs

Security

Basic needs, such as food, shelter and healthcare

walk until they drop in search of the means of survival. Refugees are men and women on the move, searching and begging for what is their right as human beings.

We in the 'First World' are made aware of these people day in, day out, on our television screens and through the first-hand reports of the young men and women who work for the Non-governmental Organisations. We watch and we read until we can bear it no longer; the sadness, the guilt and the feelings of impotence overwhelm us until we suffer from 'compassion fatigue' and return to our novels, our murder dramas or our knitting.

We are usually better at dealing with dramas nearer to home. If our neighbours' roof caves in, we take them in (although we hope it won't be for too long!). British women have knitted socks for 'our brave boys at the front' since time began, but it's harder to motivate ourselves to get organised for people we do not know. Some of us are better at donating to charity than others, but it's clearly something we should review on a regular basis. We all have our favourite charities: mine are *Médecins Sans Frontières* (for whom I might work if I am granted another life) and the Medical Foundation for the Care of Victims of Torture. Another is entitled The ShelterBox Trust, an international charity based in Cornwall, and always quick off the mark to send its boxes of tents, blankets and cooking utensils to the victims of each new disaster.

Yesterday I read of another little-known American charity. Remote Arena Medical was founded in 1985 by a British doctor, Stan Brock, initially to bring free medical care to the rural poor. This organisation recently took over the Los Angeles Forum, a vast concert venue, and turned it into an enormous field hospital for eight days. In the first two days (according to Guy Adams of the *Independent*), more than 1500 men, women and children, who could not afford to pay a doctor, received free medical care worth over £300,000. Of the doctor, Adams wrote:

> Today, Brock has no money, no income and no bank account. He spends 365 days a year at the charity events, sleeping on a small rolled-up mat on the floor and living on a diet made up entirely of porridge and fresh fruit.

What a man! Do we have here another Albert Schweitzer, I ask myself?

The second tier of Maslow's 'hierarchy' is security – in many ways a less obvious human need than food and shelter. As I understand it, Maslow is saying that we need to feel safe in order to function as human beings. In order to understand this, imagine what it must be like to know that your life is in continual danger, either from enemies or disease. Fear of death, whether it be from predators, cancer or contagion, is an all-absorbing preoccupation which makes it virtually impossible for us to concentrate on normal tasks and other people.

In times of war, or during epidemics of life-threatening illnesses, people do adapt to caring for each other, but the cost is high and the long-term toll taken great. Living in constant danger is one of the factors at the root of shell shock and post-traumatic stress, and it is a sobering fact that many of the rough-sleepers on our streets are ex-servicemen.

Although my medical work in Chile brought me into contact with malnourished babies and hungry adults, for the past thirty years or so it has been my job, my calling, to try and help men and women suffering from emotional distress. I use the term 'emotional', rather than psychological, because my work has always been with sane people who are distressed, rather than with those suffering from psychotic illness: what most people call madness.

During the twenty years that I worked with the terminally ill, I was dealing with men and women whose lives had been disrupted by disease and then the knowledge that their illness would cause their death. It would not be exaggerating to say that love was the key to this work. The 'love' of a doctor for his or her patient is a complex thing: an amalgam of diagnostic and therapeutic skills, exercised in a manner that reveals to the person that they are not only worthy of respect but also loveable. It was only when I saw an etching of a pelican feeding its young with drops of blood from its breast that I understood the cost of good palliative care. This work is demanding because there is no formula, no algorithm, for emotional and spiritual support of the dying. Yes, we must work with the truth, if that's what the person wants, but there is nothing more cruel than the truth crudely and thoughtlessly dispensed. Palliative care doctors tell the joke of the apocryphal doctor who told his dying patient not to buy any more long-playing gramophone records, but there are too many reports of blunt and unthinking information given to patients for this not to be a problem.

Talking to people about dying is not the same as telling people that they will die. Both are difficult, but the first is a dialogue, an exchange of confidences, a dance, which is at the same time a walk upon eggshells. Telling people that they will die, without first finding out what they know and understand about their illness, is violence akin to rape.

I believe that it is the exercise of the skill of empathy that makes possible the practice of loving care in any professional situation. Carl Rogers defines empathy as the ability to enter the other's world *as if* it were one's own, without losing the 'as if' quality. Empathy is a vital tool in any carer's skill-set but its use is costly; if I enter the world of the thirty-year-old mother dying of breast cancer, how can I not but feel her pain, her anger, her confusion? When I have compassion (*con-passio* – with passion), I suffer with her, but it is this knowledge that teaches me what to say and how to act; how to love. Because I feel her pain and despair, I can intuitively know what she needs me to say to her.

Important as empathy is, to have experienced in *carne propria* – in one's own flesh – what a patient is going through, is a very powerful preparation for caring. That is why so many men and women who have suffered emotionally train as counsellors, and why ex-addicts are often the best people to help those trying to 'kick the habit'.

Maslow's third tier of needs is described as social need – the need we all have for friends, for a 'confiding tie', for someone to listen to us, the need to *belong* to a group of fellow humans. Whereas the professional loving of doctors and nurses is a vital part of palliative care, indeed of all medical care, it is up to all of us to be aware of the lonely and rejected on our doorsteps. It is in this human arena that so many churches are good; the coffee served after the service is an opportunity to draw the lonely and the stranger into a warm community. Some church communities do this really well, others less so.

When I was a student at Oxford, I used to gather together those who, after Mass, were loitering at the chaplaincy door with nowhere to go, and invite them to lunch at my flat. After extracting a donation of 'half a crown' (the currency of the day), I would peddle away furiously on my bicycle to buy rice or spaghetti to make Sunday lunch. After feeding a dozen or more of my fellow students, I would sit on the floor and listen as they put the world to rights with their newly learned theology or social science. Feeding people has always been my choice of socialising and now, fifty years on, I still cook for my friends and invite the lonely and the newcomer to join us at table.

My mother was not really a sociable person, so I expect I learned to be hospitable from Michael Hollings, at whose table I was an almost daily guest. Michael, in his early days as Chaplain at Oxford, threw his house open to us students and I came to breakfast, tea and sometimes supper as well. Those of us who were regular guests soon learned to act as co-hosts, pouring tea and serving bread and jam to the shy newcomers.

The high point of Michael's hospitality was his Christmas dinner, to which he invited anyone who was alone, including myself one year (as I described in Chapter 5). In the early days of the hospice, Valerie, the matron, and I hosted Christmas dinner for any of our terminally-ill patients who were alone at home. We did it for a number of years and then our resolve weakened. Since I have retired, I have cooked dinner on Christmas night for any friends who don't want to be alone.

One of the delights of my older years has been regular contact with younger friends and colleagues. Once a fortnight, I make lunch for the three younger women who run our childhood bereavement service, Jeremiah's Journey. Joanne, the co-ordinator, has become like a daughter to me and has, for years, dog-sat my beloved Chows for two weeks each summer when I go to Maine. My other 'children' are Joe and Monique, a young couple from Scotland whom I see most days. Joe, an abseiler by profession, has had difficulty finding work locally during the recession, and it has been a delight to employ him from time to time on various odd jobs. I have recently discovered that he is a skilled and enthusiastic cook, and he is now a regular co-host when friends come to supper. He is also a precious resource in that he understands Chows and is happy to walk my stubborn beasts if I have to be elsewhere.

Caring for each other is more about listening than talking, and this has now become my professional, as well as a personal, role. In my last few years in the National Health Service, I trained as a psychotherapist and I now see around half a dozen 'clients' a week. I see men and women, the elderly, the young and those in their middle years. Initially I saw people in a small sitting room in my basement, but soon moved upstairs to my large and somewhat chaotic living room. I love being in natural light, so all aspects of my life – painting, writing, supervision and therapy – are conducted near the French windows that lead into my small terraced garden. The dogs are usually quietly in evidence, and Mollie snores in a comforting sort of way while the client and I talk and listen. It's a far cry from Freud's couch or a hospital consulting room, but none the worse, I feel, for that.

I enjoy working as a therapist more than I ever thought possible. At an intellectual level, each person's life story and problems are infinitely fascinating, while emotionally, the bonds of love and trust forged are enormously satisfying. There is also a spiritual dimension to this work that is hard to define; sometimes we talk about God, but mostly it is about relationships, both past and current. In some ways it is a priestly work: a ministering to the distressed, with an element of forgiveness and the lifting of shame, as well as a holding up of a mirror to reflect back to people traits and actions of which they may be unaware.

And lastly, to be real, what are we to do about the people who irritate us: those we dislike and those who have wronged us? The great thing about being retired is that one is no longer forced to work cheek-by-jowl with people with whom one is, frankly, incompatible. My years at the hospice were marked by such a relationship, as was my time in the Oncology department. What I did then was to keep out of that person's way and also, if I am completely truthful, 'bitched' about them behind their backs! I come from a family that didn't 'do' conflict so I have always avoided face-to-face confrontation like the plague, although I did once tell the Chairman of the Hospice Council that he was arrogant!

If I have attained any wisdom in age it has got to be this: the key is empathy! Try to understand why people are the way they are, or, as the Native American prayer goes: 'Lord, grant that I may not criticise my neighbour until I have walked a mile in his moccasins.' I find that once I have bothered to think through why people are the way they are, I am usually less irritated by their foibles.

I think that the issue of confrontation is a difficult one. Sometimes the kindest thing one can do to people is point out aspects of their behaviour that cause offence. I was sacked from my illustrious post as Medical Director at the hospice because no one dared to tell me that my frequent absences to lecture, and inevitable late arrival in the mornings, were irritating my junior colleagues beyond endurance. Had they confronted me, I would have told them that I believed my lecturing to be important and I didn't think being ten minutes late mattered. On the other hand, my dismissal was, like the proverbial ill wind, the best thing that could have happened to me, because I was given greater freedom at the hospital and was able to function in a much more innovative and creative way.

Chapter 19

Caring for Ourselves

'Love your neighbour as yourself.'
Luke 10:27

In Chapter 10 of the Gospel according to Luke, a smarty-pants lawyer
tries to catch Jesus out: 'Master,' he says, 'What must I do to inherit eternal
life?' Jesus, more than a match for him, says: 'What is written in the Law?
What do you read there?' The lawyer knows his scripture and quotes
from the God's commandments to Moses:

> 'You must love the Lord your God with all your heart, with all
> your soul, with all your strength, and with all your mind, and
> your neighbour as yourself.'

Anyone familiar with their New Testament will know that the lawyer goes
on to ask: 'And who is my neighbour?' Jesus' reply is in the form of a
parable: the story of the traveller mugged on the road to Jerusalem who is
tended by a man of different class, culture and faith. The point of the
story, of course, is that our neighbour is not the charming man next door
but the bruised and bleeding foreigner in the gutter, who may well be
playing 'possum' and about to leap on us when we attempt to help him.

My friend, the monk, would rephrase this and say that it was the
passer-by who was neighbour to the wounded man. Be that as it may, my
purpose is to explore a rather ignored part of this story: the statement
that we should love our neighbours as we love ourselves! The question
here is not 'Who is our neighbour?', or 'How should we love her?', but:
'How do we love ourselves?'

Love of self has got a pretty bad press over the years and, in religious circles, has often been equated with conceit, greed and selfishness. I see far more clients, however, who have been taught to hate themselves, than I do those inflated with self-love. My intention in this chapter, therefore, is to explore the meaning and the importance of loving and caring for ourselves.

As I write these words, I hear, as if it were yesterday, the voice of my psychotherapist Jim Drewery, as he exclaimed, in an exasperated voice: 'You are destroying yourself!' He was right; I was. I was injuring, if not destroying, myself, by trying, single-handed, to save the oppressed people of Chile. By this I mean that I was lecturing most weekends, at human rights events; I was, by telling again and again the story of my torture and imprisonment in Chile, trying to shock and blackmail people into caring about Chile. I remember, that same year, consulting a psychiatrist for insomnia and depression. After I had told him of my frenetic work and lecture schedule, he looked at me through his steel-rimmed spectacles and asked me quietly: 'Why do you do it?' I was amazed, nonplussed and furious; how could he not *see* that I was 'Chile's Angel', a latter-day Joan of Arc, called by name to bring down the military junta and save the prisoners I had left behind!

My problem then, was not that I didn't love myself, but that I thought my 'call' made me super-human. I don't think I believed this at an intellectual level, because I was not actually deranged, just driven by my own expectations of myself and the demands of my cause. I was very fond at that time of quoting to myself a prayer attributed to St Ignatius of Loyola, which went something like this:

> Lord Jesus, teach me to be generous,
> To give and not to count the cost;
> To fight and not to heed the wounds
> To work and not to seek for rest
> Safe in the knowledge that I do Thy most holy will.

I still find this prayer seductive. I want to be hard working and generous, surprise, surprise, because I want to be loved! My problem (as it was then) of overwork and failure to care for my self is a very common one, especially among people who work for the sick and the needy. Most of us can do it in times of emergency – flood, fire, war, the twin towers disaster – but working to capacity over the long term ends in tears and burn out.

Absurdly, this pattern of work is a kind of conceit: we think we are stronger or holier than our colleagues, and forget we are human with human needs. One of the problems with doctors is that we, of the older generation, were brought up to work sixty to a hundred hours a week. It was my proud boast, in my early years as Medical Director of the Hospice, that I worked a hundred hours a week and was paid for nineteen! It is no surprise to me now, when I look back, that I couldn't sleep, was depressed and suffered from anxiety and the occasional panic attack.

Although I no longer lecture about occupational stress, I still see patients who suffer from it. As I listen to their stories, I have Maslow's list of needs at the back of my mind. First and foremost, does this person get enough rest? Does he eat a reasonable diet (so many people don't)? Does she take any exercise? Does he have any friends and, if so, does he spend 'quality' time with them and his family? If she has creative gifts, such as painting, writing or music, is she using them and developing them? I have come to believe that if men and women neglect their creative gifts, they suffer emotionally and their lives are the poorer for it.

Before I embark upon my account of how I believe we should look after ourselves, it seems logical to answer the rather cynical question: *Why bother?* Although few people actually articulate this question in as many words, many treat their minds and bodies as if their behaviour will have no consequences. If a farmer treated his animals, or a racing driver his car, in the way some of us treat ourselves, the RSPCA and the Society for the Nurture of Cars would call them to task!

There are a number of very obvious practical medical reasons why we should care for ourselves, and some less obvious philosophical or spiritual ones. As you (I assume) and I are spiritual people, let's start with those. This leads me immediately to a deeply philosophical question: Do we own our bodies and our minds?

Religious, especially Roman Catholic, language is rich with pious phrases such as 'your body is the temple of the Holy Spirit', and notions such as guarding our virginity for our 'Spiritual Bridegroom'. If we believe, as I do, that we are created by God, do we belong to her? Are our minds and bodies, as it were, on loan to us for the duration of our lives? Is suicide an affront to the Divine? Remember that it is not so many years ago that suicide 'victims' could not be buried in 'hallowed (consecrated) ground'. Another very topical issue is the question of euthanasia: Is helping a terminally ill person to die murder? Or is it the ultimate act of compassion to the dying?

Then, of course, there is the relationship between a mother and her unborn child. Our society believes that a mother has the right to end the life of an unwanted foetus. What does God think about that? (We know what the Right to Life groups think.) When I was a medical student, fifty years ago, Catholic teaching decreed that if there was a clinical situation in which the delivery of a baby put the mother's life at risk, the birth could still proceed. There was no question of killing the baby in order to save the mother's life, not even if the baby was deformed and the mother had ten dependent children. The classical situation in which doctors chose to kill the baby to save the mother was that of an obstructed labour in which the baby was hydrocephalic (the baby's head was greatly swollen with excess brain fluid and could not pass through the birth canal). I remember being taught that the obstetrician should pierce the baby's skull so that the fluid drained out and the birth could proceed. If this was not done, the mother would continue in a fruitless obstructed labour until she and the baby both died.

Times, of course, are very different now: we have scans to examine the baby throughout the pregnancy and vulnerable babies are delivered by Caesarean section. We are still left, however, with the dilemma of whether to terminate a pregnancy if the foetus is abnormal. I find it interesting, even as I write, to note how the use of technical medical language reduces the emotional impact. To speak of an abnormal foetus is less distressing than to say that the *baby* is deformed. To 'terminate a pregnancy' is easier to say than kill an unborn baby.

I am not saying that I believe that termination of a pregnancy, the killing of an unborn baby, is always wrong. While it is always tragic to end a life, sometimes, rarely, it is the lesser of two evils. I am thinking here of the situation I described earlier (mercifully now rare), where to proceed with a pregnancy would put the mother's life at grave risk. There are, of course, many, many situations where pregnancies are unwanted; for example, a child conceived by rape, or a pregnancy in a very young girl of, say, thirteen years. Much will depend in these situations upon the emotional health of the mother, and I do not feel able to legislate in such complex situations.

❦

At the other end of life, the issue of euthanasia in a terminally ill adult is more in my area of expertise. There is no doubt that there have been enormous advances in pain and symptom control for cancer patients since the Hospice Movement became established in the United Kingdom from the 1950s onward. The majority of terminally ill men and women suffering from cancer can be kept reasonably comfortable until they die. There are, however, other diseases which are sometimes more distressing than cancer, such as motor neurone disease and other conditions causing paralysis of limbs, swallowing and breathing apparatus. How are we to judge – indeed, how dare we judge – individuals who feel that their life is so terrible that they wish to end it? 'If he was a dog, you'd have him put down!' is the classic comment made by distressed bystanders, whether friends, relatives or carers.

There has been a lot of discussion about assisted suicide at time of writing this book, and there are many good people both for and against it. For me, the most difficult issue is the impact of such assisted deaths upon those who do the assisting, and those who are left behind. For those who die, the pain is soon over, for better or for worse, but for those who remain there will always be painful soul-searching and often guilt. If this were a medical article on the subject I would need to refer to the 'Dutch Experience', and the statistics from the situations in the USA, where assisted suicide is legal. One of the familiar arguments against legalising 'mercy killing' is that it will be the beginning of the 'slippery slope', that it will become common practice and greedy relatives will put pressure on the frail elderly to request an end to their lives.

My question in this chapter, however, is not: Is it morally wrong to help someone to die? But: 'How do we perceive God's attitude to the patient, to the person who wishes to end his or her life?

'Who can know the mind of God?' is the quotation that springs instantly to mind, though it took me a while to locate it. St Paul seems to be quoting Isaiah when he exclaims, in Romans 11:34: 'Who could ever know the mind of the Lord? Who could even be his counsellor?'

Chapter 40 of Isaiah (a version other than Chapter 6 which includes the 'call of the prophet') is a glorious poem of tribute to the power and transcendence of God. The reader will likely find much of it familiar:

> All flesh is grass
> and its beauty like the wild flowers.
> The grass withers. The flower fades
> when the breath of Yahweh blows on them.

(The grass is without doubt the people)
The grass withers, the flower fades,
But the word of our God remains forever.
Isaiah 40:6–8

I find these words almost unbearably poignant; a friend of mine has just died and I have watched her fade from boundless energy and beauty, through illness and hope of recovery, to a sad acceptance of her impending death. When told that she had only a few weeks to live she arranged a farewell party, a sort of living wake. Two hundred people came to honour her life and hug her for the last time. When everyone was gathered she appeared, garlanded in flowers like a bride. Then, alas, for her, the weeks turned into months and sadly she lay waiting and longing for it to be over; to put it bluntly, longing to die.

I think most people find long drawn-out terminal illness difficult, and I can understand why some people ask to be helped to die. I have never done it; it is against medical ethics, and against the law, but people still ask.

Towards the end of Isaiah 40, the prophet proclaims the mystery and the majesty of the Divine. It is here that we find the passage quoted by St Paul:

Who could have advised the spirit of Yahweh
what counsellor could have instructed him?
Whom has he consulted to enlighten him,
and to learn the path of justice
and discover the most skilful ways.
Isaiah 40:13–14

It goes on:

To whom could you liken God?
What image could you contrive of Him?
Did you not know?
Had you not heard?
Yahweh is an everlasting God,
He created the boundaries of the earth.
He does not grow tired or weary,
His understanding is beyond fathoming.
Isaiah 40:25, 28

167

Anthony de Mello, an Indian Jesuit priest who died some years ago, is quoted as saying: 'Empty out your teacup, God.' I wonder if our notion of God is too human, too small, when we imagine that he would be angry if one of his creatures found life so intolerable that she chose to die rather than continue living? I would quote you once again the wise old hymn, which declares:

> There's wideness in God's mercy
> Like the wideness of the sea;
> There's a kindness in his justice,
> Which is more than liberty.
> For the love of God is broader
> Than the measure of our mind;
> And the heart of the Eternal
> Is most wonderfully kind.
>
> F. W. Faber

This may not be your notion of God, but it is surely mine and I do not believe in a God who would condemn any man or woman so distressed that he or she chose to die.

That, then, is my notion of Divine Judgement on mercy killing. It is not, however, the law's view, nor, interestingly enough, the view of those who speak for the palliative care doctors. Their argument is that it is nearly always possible to control distressing symptoms in the dying and we should work to improve the care of our patients rather than sanction a law that may be abused.

When I began this chapter, I had no intention of dealing with these contentious issues. I set out, in fact, to write about overwork and stress and over-indulgence in food, alcohol and drugs. There is, of course, an abundance of literature on all these subjects, so I resolved to contain my enthusiasm and try not to get carried away.

Now that I try to explore the subject, however, I find myself absurdly lost for words. How can I lay down the law about stress and overwork when I too have worked too hard and suffered burnout and depression? How can I recommend that you eat your 'five portions of fruit and veg a day' when I know that I only manage it because I can afford blackberries, raspberries and pineapple? I'm quite sure I wouldn't finish up my greens if they were cauliflower or overcooked cabbage! I *do* believe that adult men and women are responsible for their health; that they should not eat too much, drink too much or take mind-altering substances. But I know too how easy it is to have another piece of chocolate, another glass of wine and to be the rueful possessor of a spare tyre.

It is really only since I have retired and had my dogs that I take any exercise worth mentioning, and it is only in the past two months that I have managed to lose a stone and drop two clothes sizes. There are so many reasons why people fail to care for themselves, not least ignorance, stress, poverty and depression. All we can do is learn how to look after ourselves in the sure and certain knowledge that, if we don't, someone else will have to do it for us. Humility, discipline and restraint are not popular virtues, but unless we practice them we will find ourselves unfit to help each other.

Much of what I have written in the last few pages is, of course, relevant to my own culture, my own world. What relevance do humility and discipline have in Darfur and Somalia? As John Harriott writes with such power in 'Our World':

> Here men banqueting grandly
> on foods flown from the corner of the globe.
> There men killing for a scrap of bread.
> Here men clamouring for money to buy luxuries;
> there men desperate for pennies to keep alive 'til dusk.
> Here the best of doctors, clinics, nurses;
> there pain without relief,
> disease without a remedy
> death without a struggle.

I am once again brought back, full circle, to the issue of stewardship of my resources and charitable giving. 'You're eligible for a loan you know,' said the cashier when I took some more money out of my already overdrawn account. 'But I've *got* a loan,' I said. 'I know,' she said, 'but you could top it up.' Temptation! Temptation! How difficult it is to balance one's wants and needs and 'shoulds' against a finite income. My budgeting is made particularly complicated by the intermittent nature of my income and my ever-present delight in shopping of any kind! My only saving grace is that I delight in using and wearing other people's unwanted goods, so if I can confine myself to the charity shops I won't have to 'top up' my loan!

Chapter 20

Caring for God

'You must love the Lord your God with all your heart, with all your soul, with all your strength, and with all your mind, and your neighbour as yourself.'

Luke 10:27

Having recently quoted these words of the lawyer who answered Jesus' query as to what he read in the Law, I assumed that I would find them in the Ten Commandments; but I didn't. The Commandments are very clear that we should not worship graven images of the Divine (idols), but nowhere that I could find do they actually tell us to *love* God. The Old Testament tells us again and again, however, that Yahweh is a 'jealous' God and that he will tolerate no rivals:

You shall bow down to no other god, for Yahweh's name is the Jealous One: he is a jealous God.

Exodus 34:14

It is tempting to understand this 'jealous' God as a possessive, domineering father or lover: the traditional figure of the old man with a long white beard. Indeed, that seems to be what the Israelites 'projected' on to the God hidden in the cloud on Mount Sinai. It is fascinating to read the account of the promise of the Covenant in Exodus 19. The Israelites, as we know, fled from Egypt, a pitiful bunch of refugees with their scant possessions, their children and their animals. They were simple people, nomads of the wilderness, without Moses' intellectual sophistication from his court upbringing, and they came from a tradition which taught them that El Shaddai, the God of the Mountain, was to be greatly feared.

It was for this reason that they clung to their 'household gods', their graven images, for comfort.

After three days preparation, Moses led the people out of the camp to meet God; they stood at the bottom of the mountain, expectantly, and no doubt a little nervous. Then it began:

> The mountain of Sinai was entirely wrapped in smoke, because Yahweh had descended on it in the form of a fire. Like smoke from a furnace, the smoke went up and the whole mountain shook violently. Louder and louder grew the sound of the trumpet. Moses spoke and God answered him in peals of thunder.
>
> Exodus 19:18–19

It sounds to me like a volcanic eruption, or at least a terrible storm, and it's hardly surprising that the people were scared witless.

' "Speak to us yourself," they said to Moses, "and we will listen; but do not let God speak to us or we shall die" ' (20:19). So Moses went up into the dark cloud where God was, and the people stayed below, wetting themselves with fear. I thought it was just three days that Moses spent with God, but no, it was forty days and forty nights. No wonder the people despaired and pressured Aaron to make them something tangible to worship: a graven image, the famous golden calf.

At this moment, let us interest ourselves, not in the weakness of the people but in what Moses was learning from his forty day 'retreat', his encounter with the Divine. Yahweh was terrifying, that goes without saying. But what kept Moses up that mountain for more than one month? True, God was giving him the Ten Commandments with all the small print, but that was just a by-product of the meeting; what was really happening was that Moses was entering into a relationship with Yahweh. They were bonding, the way a mother does with her child or a man with his wife. I'm not talking about sex here, but about something infinitely more powerful: the fusing, the union of a man's spirit with his God.

When he came down from the mountain, we are told: 'Moses' face shone. He did not know that the skin on his face was radiant after speaking with Yahweh' (34:29). It was so incandescent that the sight of it scared the people and Moses had to cover his face with a veil, which he only removed when he returned to speak with Yahweh.

Moses developed such a degree of intimacy with God that one day he asked an unthinkable favour. Moses said: 'Show me your glory, I beg you'

(33:18). It is prudent to explain here (biblical scholars will excuse me) what is meant by God's Glory. The footnotes in my Jerusalem Bible tell me that the glory of Yahweh is the manifestation of God's presence. On Sinai, the 'glory' is expressed as a flame, as it was in the burning bush, while, for the Hebrews in the wilderness, God was manifest as a 'pillar of cloud by day and a fire by night'. Another image, that of a brilliant light (which left its imprint on Moses' face) is said to stand for 'Gods inapproachable majesty'. Here we have a divine paradox: the God of the mountain is so awesome that no man can see his face and live (33:20). Yet he is prepared to show himself to his faithful disciples; in this case, Moses.

God said: 'I will let all my splendour pass in front of you, and I will pronounce before you the name of Yahweh' (by pronouncing his name, God reveals something of himself to Moses) (33:19). There follows the fascinating description of the event in which God places Moses 'in a cleft of the rock' and shields him with his hand while his Glory passes by. Then, wonder of wonders, God takes away his hand so that Moses may see his 'back parts', for his face is not to be seen.

We are all too familiar with the denial and longing which characterise our pursuit of the Divine, but we are the beneficiaries of Moses' audacity, of what Yahweh revealed about himself. When Moses asked him,

> Yahweh passed before him and proclaimed: 'Yahweh, Yahweh, a
> God of tenderness and compassion, slow to anger, rich in
> kindness and faithfulness; for thousands he maintains his
> kindness, forgives faults, transgression, sin; yet he lets nothing
> go unchecked, punishing the father's fault in the sons and in the
> grandsons to the third and fourth generation.'
>
> Exodus 34:6–7

It is in this moment that God reveals to Moses why he is loveable; not only is he terrifyingly beautiful and all-powerful, but he is tender and compassionate, kind and forgiving. I suppose one could say, simplistically, that God is really scary but once you get to know her, you can only love her. If calling God 'her' upsets you, by all means revert to he, but ask yourself why the all-powerful creator of the Universe could not be feminine. It is interesting, in this context, to look at the Book of Wisdom, in which King Solomon goes into raptures in praise of this mysterious quality of the Divine:

> She is a breath of the power of God,
> pure emanation of the glory of the Almighty;
> hence nothing impure can find a way into her.
> She is a reflection of the eternal light,
> untarnished mirror of God's active power,
> image of his goodness.
>
> Wisdom 7:25–26

Is wisdom the feminine part of God? (Does God *need* a feminine part, you may ask?) Further on in this book, we see Wisdom as the all-powerful yet kindly creator:

> For your great strength is always at your call;
> who can withstand the might of your arm?
> In your sight the whole world is like a grain of dust that tips the scales,
> like a drop of morning dew falling on the ground.
> Yet you are merciful to all, because you can do all things,
> and overlook men's sins so they can repent.
> Yes, you love all that exists, you hold nothing of what you have made in abhorrence,
> for had you hated anything, you would not have formed it.
>
> Wisdom 11:21–24

Who, we might well ask, is Wisdom? The footnotes in my Jerusalem Bible tell me that from Emperor Justin onwards, Christian tradition in its development of Trinitarian doctrine has almost always identified the Wisdom of the passage above with the Word. St Paul (who never met the man Jesus) speaks lyrically of Christ:

> He is the image of the unseen God and the first born of all creation,
> for in him were created all things in heaven and on earth:
> everything visible and everything invisible, Thrones,
> Dominations, Sovereignties, Powers – all things were created
> through him and for him.
>
> Colossians 1:15–16

God, El Shaddai, Yahweh, the Holy One, the Creator, the Divine, Wisdom, Jesus of Nazareth, Jesus Christ, the Word of God: is it any wonder we get confused?! The Triune God, the Three in One, or the Blessed

Trinity, are very hard concepts to grasp and my guess is that the scholars have many different thoughts. I am no theologian, though I have rubbed shoulders with quite a few, but I find no need to understand the intricacies of 'who begot whom'. These days, as always, I believe in a Creator God who holds the whole world in his 'hands'. So far, so good; most primitive peoples believe this, which is why they pray, make offerings and sacrifice their animals. Where I, and many people like me, differ, is that I believe this God is good and kind and merciful and he loves me more than I can understand. This God invites me to enter into a relationship with him and, in my simple-minded way, I have done just that.

This was not a one-off conversion experience, nor have I 'accepted Jesus Christ as my Saviour'. I am not a 'Born-again Christian' and I must admit to feeling very uncomfortable with the concept. Occasionally people ask me if I have been 'saved', and I don't really know what to say because I just don't use that sort of language.

I feel infinitely more comfortable, for example, with the language of Psalm 62:

> O God, you are my God, for you I long;
> for you my soul is thirsting.
> My body pines for you
> like a dry, weary land without water.
> So I gaze on you in the sanctuary
> to see your strength and your glory.
> For your love is better than life,
> my lips will speak your praise,
> so I will bless you all my life,
> in your name I will lift up my hands.
> My soul shall be filled as with a banquet
> my mouth shall praise you with joy.
>
> Psalm 62:1–5

'Your love is better than life': what a crazy statement this is by human standards, and yet, throughout the ages, men and women have gone singing to their deaths for this same love.

I find this mysterious personal relationship with the Divine extremely difficult to write about, but, when I read what others have written, I can say: 'Ah! Yes! That's it!'

Most of the writing which strikes such a chord with me is poetry; not only Christian verse, but also that of some of the Eastern Mystics, such as the fourteenth-century Sufi, Hafiz.

There is a book of the poetry of Hafiz, translated by Daniel Ladinsky, which has the wonderful title *I Heard God Laughing*. I love the light-hearted touch of his writing; for example, Hafiz tells us that 'the Beloved's nature is pure Joy. The closer we come to Him, the more we are able to hear and feel God's laughter.' 'The rhythm of His Laughter is the music of the dance of life,' says Ladinsky, 'That music is the essence of Love, and it is the radiant core of every song of Hafiz.'

Here is a fragment of Ladinsky's translation of 'A Tethered Falcon':

> My heart sits on the Arm of God
> Like a tethered falcon
> Suddenly unhooded.
> I am now blessedly crazed
> Because my Master's Astounding Effulgence
> Is in constant view.
>
> My piercing eyes,
> Which have searched every world
> For Tenderness and Love, Now lock on the Royal Target –
> The Wild Holy One
> Whose Beauty illuminates Existence.
> My soul endures a magnificent longing.

I love his wild language and imagery, which recalls to my mind, yet again, Gerard Manley Hopkins's masterpiece, 'The Windhover':

I caught this morning morning's minion, kingdom
of daylight's dauphin, dapple-dawn-drawn Falcon, in his riding
Of the rolling level underneath him steady air, and striding
High there, how he rung upon the rein of a wimpling wing
In his ecstasy! then off, off forth on swing,
As a skate's heel sweeps smooth on a bow-bend: the hurl and gliding
Rebuffed the big wind. My heart in hiding
Stirred for a bird – the achieve of; the mastery of the thing!

It seems to matter little that, for Hopkins, the falcon is an image of Christ while, for Hafiz, the bird is his heart. Poetic images in both the scriptures and spiritual poetry run one into the other until they merge like water-colours on paper. This fluidity was something I found particularly hard to grasp when I made the quantum leap from the certainty of science to the imagery of the Old Testament. It was only when I let go of the desire to analyse each word and sentence that I began to understand the whole.

Although the mystery of a man or woman's relationship with the Divine is best expressed in the language of poetry, the way that relationship is achieved and nurtured needs to be spelled out clearly. The first thing to say is that our relationship with God is always pure gift. We do not find God like the pearl in the field, but, rather, God finds us. Francis Thompson's famous poem, 'The Hound of Heaven', portrays the soul in desperate flight from its Creator:

> I fled Him, down the nights and down the days;
> I fled Him, down the arches of the years;
> I fled Him, down the labyrinthine ways
> Of my own mind; and in the midst of tears
> I hid from Him, and under running laughter.
> Up vistaed hopes I sped;
> And shot, precipitated,
> Adown Titanic glooms of chasmed fears,
> From those strong Feet that followed, followed after.
> But with unhurrying chase,
> And unperturbéd pace,
> Deliberate speed, majestic instancy,
> They beat – and a Voice beat
> More instant than the Feet –
> 'All things betray thee, who betrayest Me.'

I used to identify with this poem for so many anguished years when I thought that God was calling me to be a nun, for, like Thompson in his second verse:

> (For, though I knew His love Who followèd,
> Yet was I sore adread
> Lest, having Him, I must have naught beside.)

I was brought up to believe that the Religious Life and the Priesthood were the only way of life for a man or woman who, like the rich young man in the Gospels, wanted to follow Christ, to love God with all his or her heart and mind and soul. How wrong I was. The Gospels are so simple that we miss the point. 'Love one another as I have loved you,' says Jesus in his Last Supper discourse. What God wants in return for his love of us is that we should love one another, especially the *anawim* – the poor, the hurt, the needy and the broken-hearted. He spelled it out, oh, so clearly, in his description of the Last Judgement:

'I was hungry and you gave me food;
I was thirsty and you gave me drink;
I was a stranger and you made me welcome;
Naked and you clothed me,
Sick and you visited me,
In prison and you came to see me.'
                                    Matthew 25:35–36

These corporal works of mercy are both the pre-requisites of a relation-ship with our God and also a fruit of that same relationship. By obeying the Commandments, by following Christ, we become acquainted with God, and once we know him, we want nothing else. Along with loving one another by kindness and sharing, we find that following Christ demands a high degree of integrity: the Truth does indeed set us free.

In practical terms, I understand this to mean that the spiritual woman does not fiddle her taxes and, when she finds that she has been given too much change, she takes it back to the shop. (On the other hand, when she finds a gold coin smiling up at her through the grass in the park, she pockets it without a qualm and thanks God for her beneficence!)

The very public scandals in which our Members of Parliament in the UK have been found to be 'creative' with their expenses is an example of how the spiritual man or woman should not behave. We would do well to print on our T-shirts, if not on our hearts, the famous words of the prophet Micah:

This is what Yahweh asks of you, only this:
That you act Justly,
Love tenderly, and walk humbly with your God.
                                    Micah 6:8

The last thing that needs addressing in my chapter about Caring for God is prayer; or, as I like to think of it, 'wasting time with God'. I think it was Cyril of Alexandria who described prayer as 'keeping company with God'. So how can I do better than choose a doctor of the Church? There is a sense, of course, in which we are never out of God's sight; we are always in his all-present, all-powerful company. As the Psalmist puts it so clearly, God's hand is always upon us:

O where can I go from your spirit,
or where can I flee from your face?
If I climb the heavens, you are there.
If I lie in the grave, you are there.

If I take the wings of the dawn
and dwell at the sea's furthest end,
even there your hand would lead me,
your right hand would hold me fast.

For it was you who created my being,
knit me together in my mother's womb.
I thank you for the wonder of my being,
for the wonders of all your creation.
Psalm 139:7–10, 13–14

Ours is an Everywhere God, we cannot escape him, so why then do we try to ignore him, pretend he has nothing to do with us? The intuition of my childhood, in which it seemed more logical to go to church every day *except* Sunday, rather than vice versa, was not far out. The only logical way to behave is to acknowledge God's presence throughout each and every day.

Before you panic, or write me off as a religious nut, let me say more about prayer, or our communication with the Divine. The most comforting thing I ever read on this subject was a remark by a Benedictine monk of Downside Abbey, Dom John Chapman: 'Pray as you can, he said, not as you can't!' Surely this is the most liberating thing ever said about prayer? Don't worry if you can't stand church, he says. Don't worry if charismatic worship turns you off. Don't worry! Be at peace and do it your way.

If you think about it, there are more ways of worshipping the Divine than there are psalms in the Psalter or beads on your rosary. The Buddhists do it meditating, some in the lotus position and some not. Some do it watching the breath, others by reciting a mantra. Muslims pray on their mats facing Mecca, while the Whirling Dervishes dance themselves into frenzy. Irish Catholics pray to the Virgin, counting the paters and the aves on their beads. Benedictine monks chant the psalms half a dozen times a day, as do Dominican Friars if they can spare the time. And I? What do I do? Well, I have practised all the above, except the Sufi dancing, at different times of my life. As a child, I went to Mass and

Benediction and sat silently in the boarder's chapel in my dressing gown before I went to bed. As a medical student, I cycled to Mass every day, more because I loved the Chaplain than through devotion. When I qualified, I learned to pray on the hoof, baptising aborted foetuses under the operating room tap and pretending the corridors were a cloister. Then I gave the whole thing up for about ten years, during an intense friendship with an atheist. From her I learned about the poor, injustice and the struggle for human rights; so I reckon I wasn't that far from God.

Since then, I've been in prison, in a monastery, in a convent, in a hospice and then in a hospital. At one particularly disciplined time, I prayed for an hour a day in the dark, sitting cross-legged in front of a candle.

Now, alas, I can't sit cross-legged anymore, so I sit on the sofa for half an hour with a cup of tea and abandon myself to God, while scratching the dogs' backs. Are you appalled? And do I care? I have always prayed better with a cup of something hot, and I like to think the dog massage is my version of a rosary or prayer wheel.

That prayer time can be quite distracted, as all the things I have to do that day tend to crowd into my consciousness. Mostly, however, I ignore them and, as this is God's time, I don't act on anything until it's over. I use few words, just a fragment of psalms or prayer if it comes to me.

This kind of prayer is about being still in both mind and body, and I am probably at my stillest later in the morning as I sit at the sea's edge with my coffee and the dogs chill out at my side. The sea invites that still gaze into the middle distance, which brings a blessed quiet to mind and heart.

This praying without words is something that is woven into my life. It comes and goes throughout the day, like the waves upon the beach. This is my way; but it may not be yours.

'Pray as you can: not as you can't.' Read a prayer book, chant a mantra, say the Rosary, sing a hymn. Whatever 'works' for you is 'your way'. Jesus said somewhere: 'By their fruits ye shall know them,' so check out your harvest from time to time.

Hopefully, you are each day a little kinder, a little more honest and a little more patient? If you are that, if you forget everything else, remember that ours is an Everywhere God who loves us, whoever we are and whatever we do.

All she asks is that we love one another as she has loved us; that we care for the world in which we live, for the people and the creatures who live in it with us, and for ourselves.

Lastly, that we care for the God who laid down his own life that we might have it more abundantly.